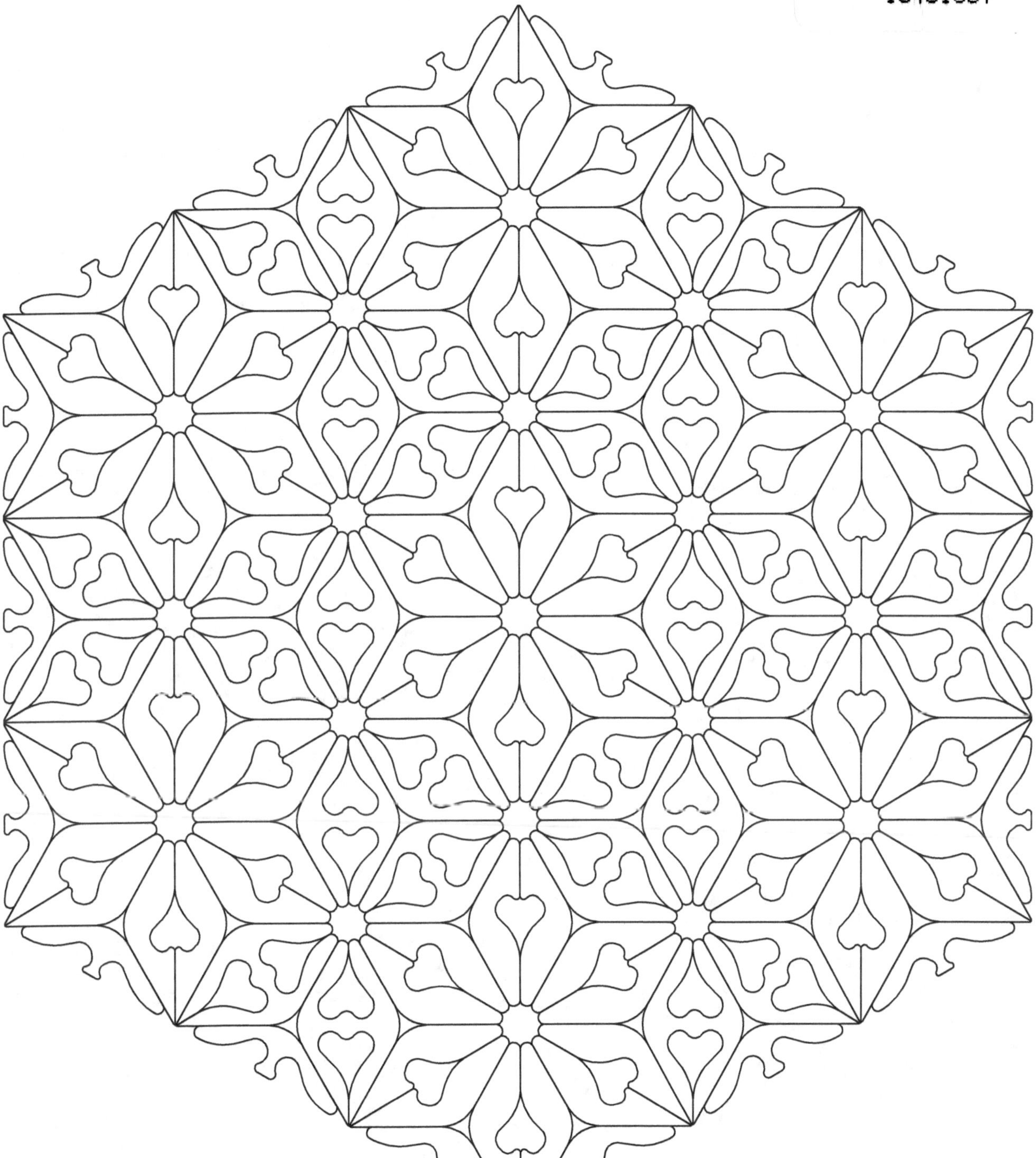

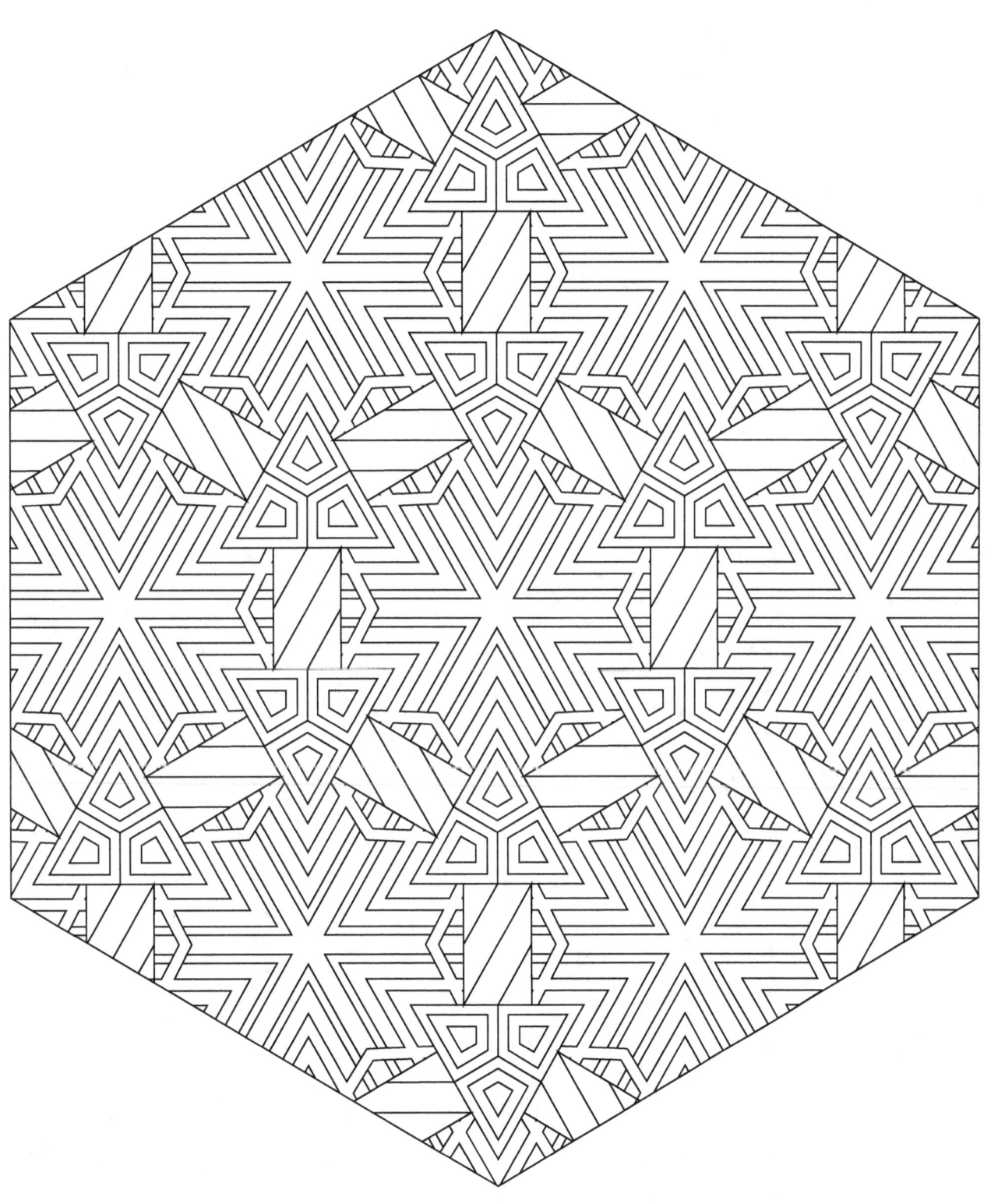

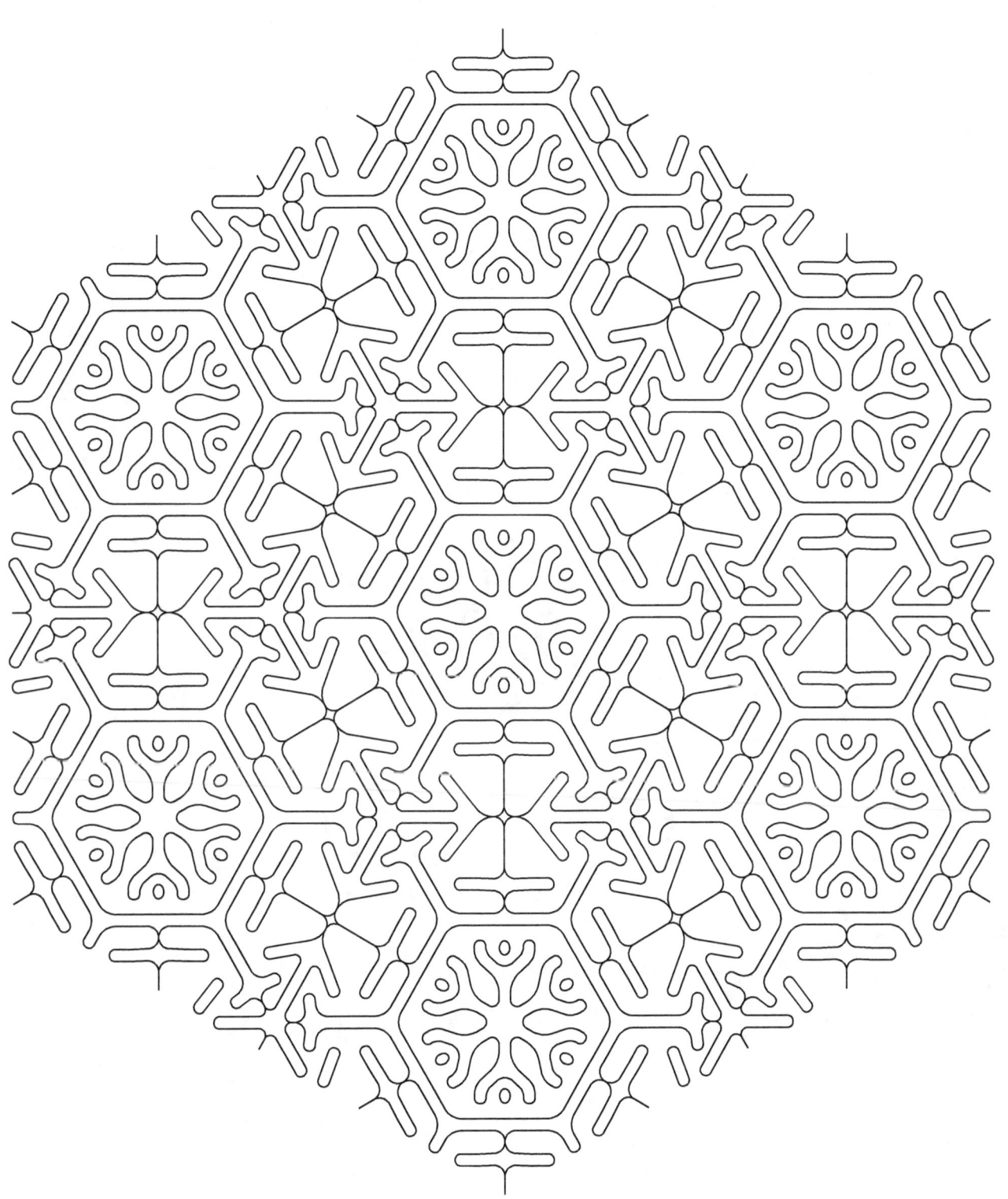

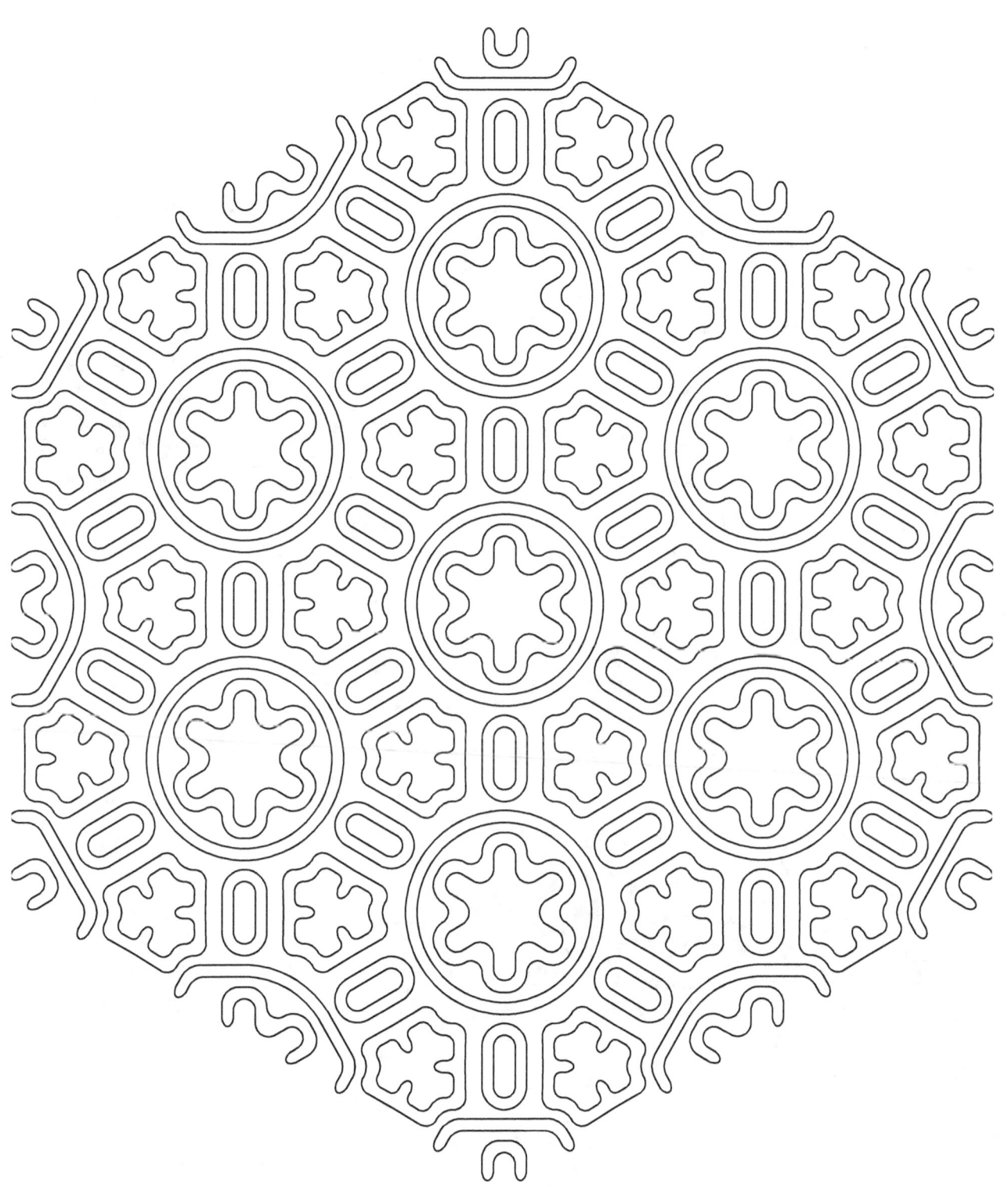

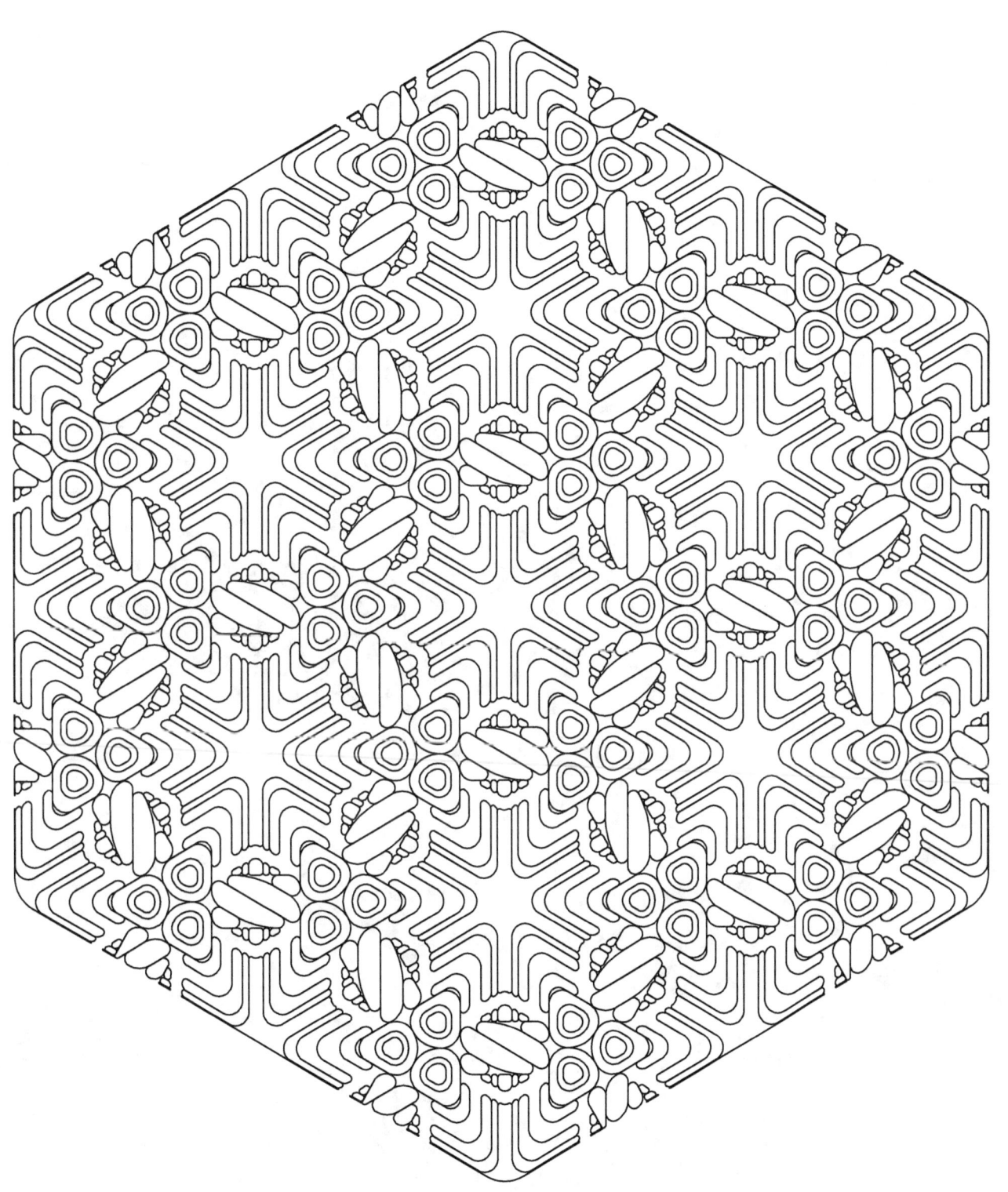

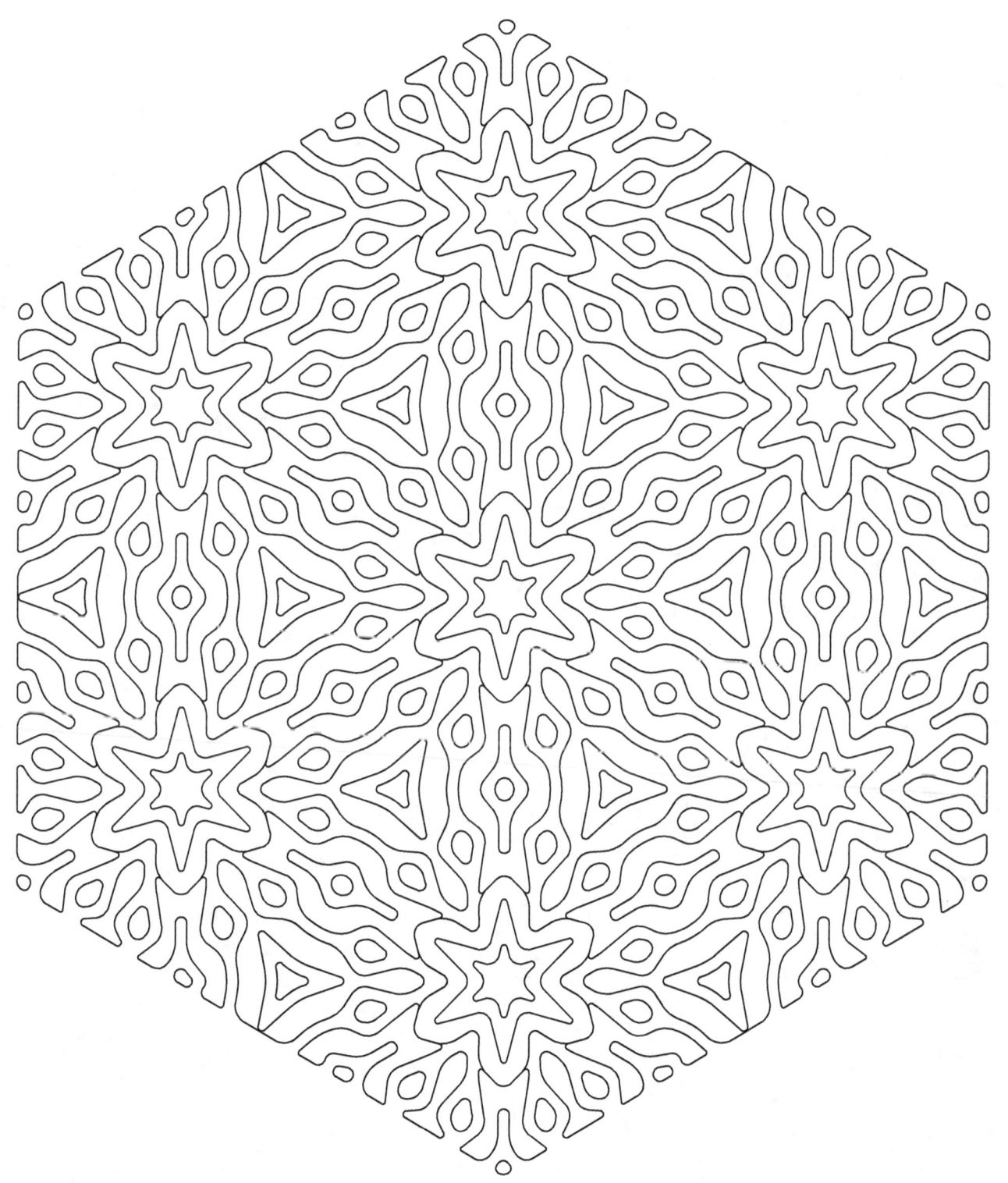

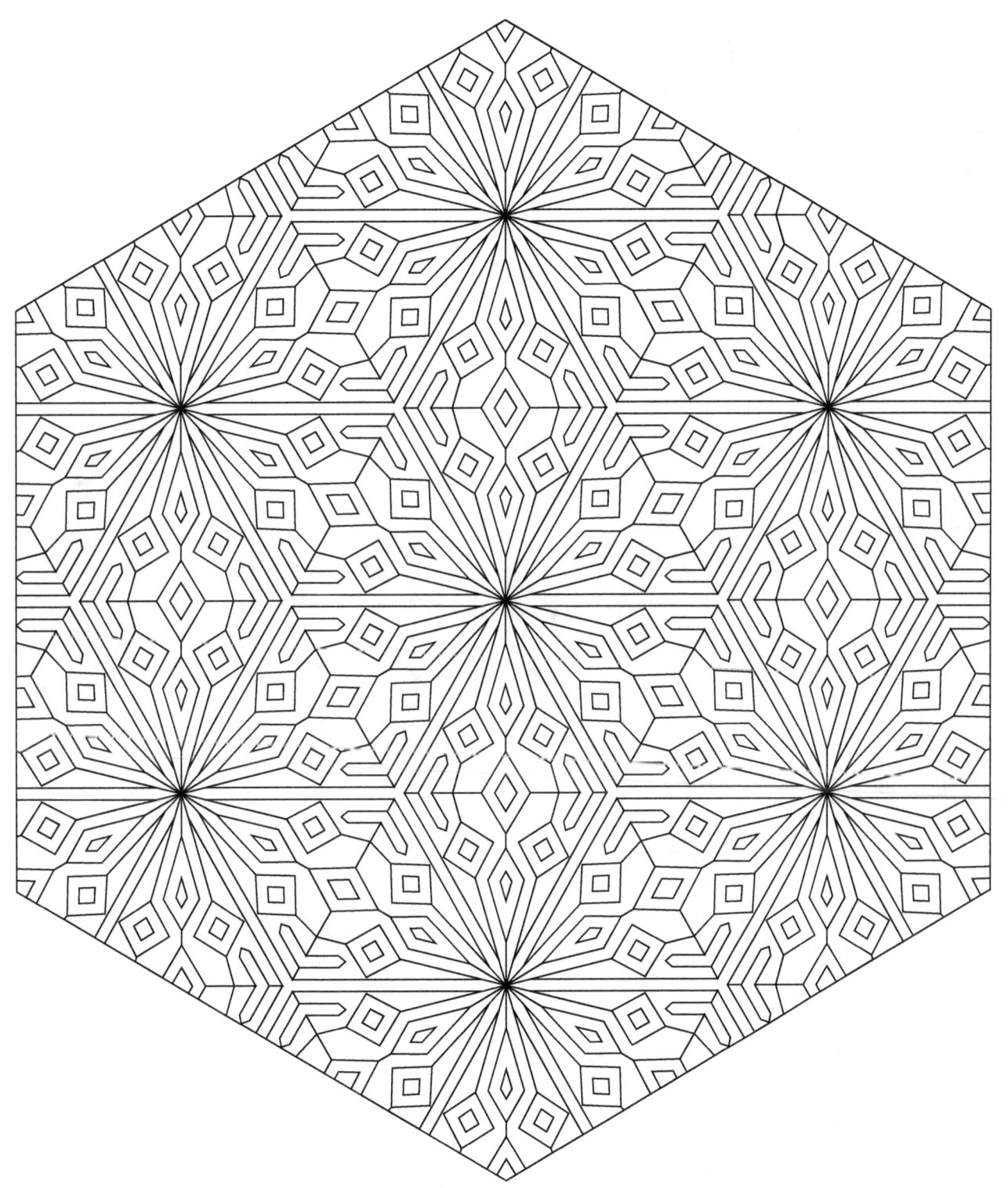

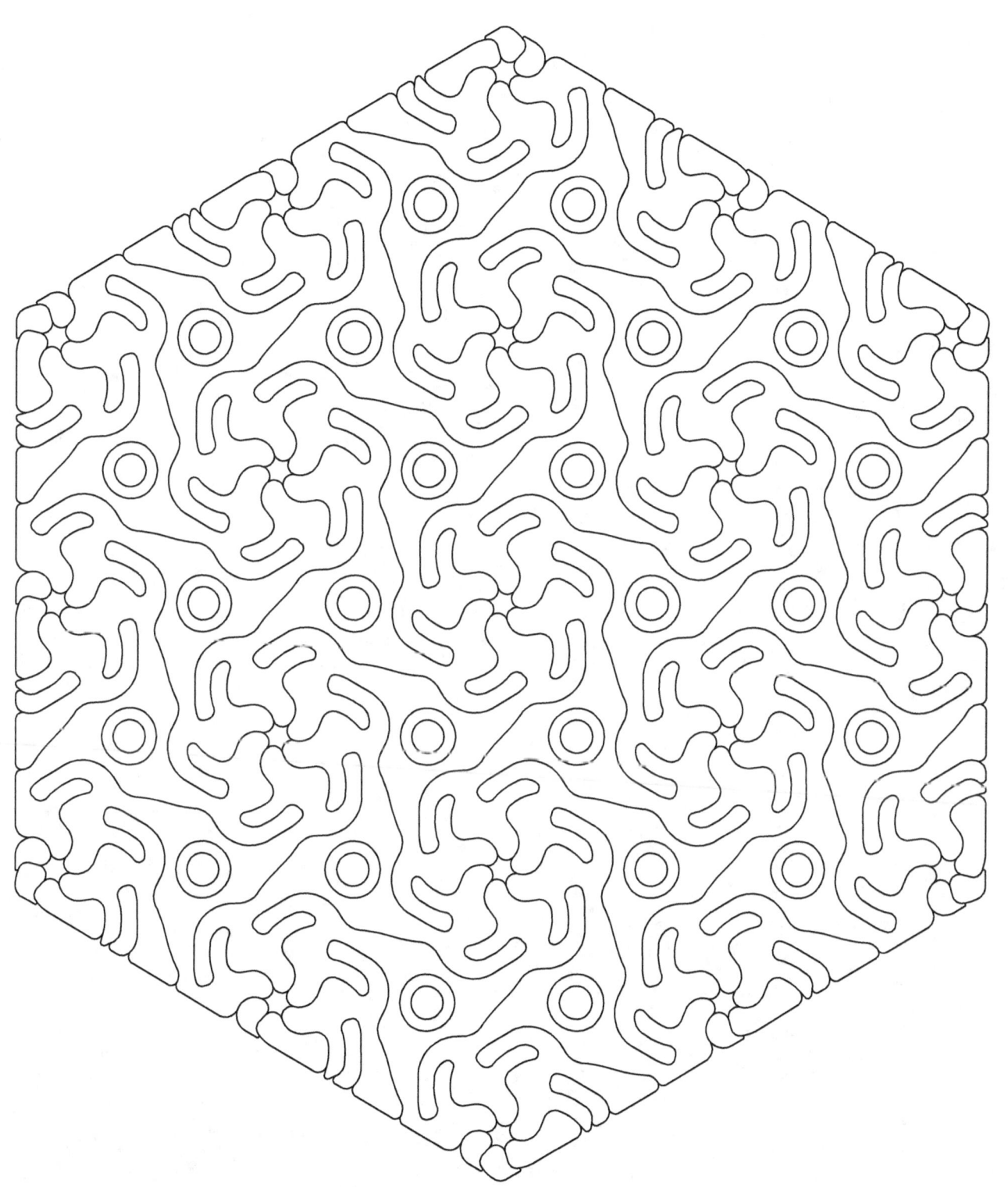

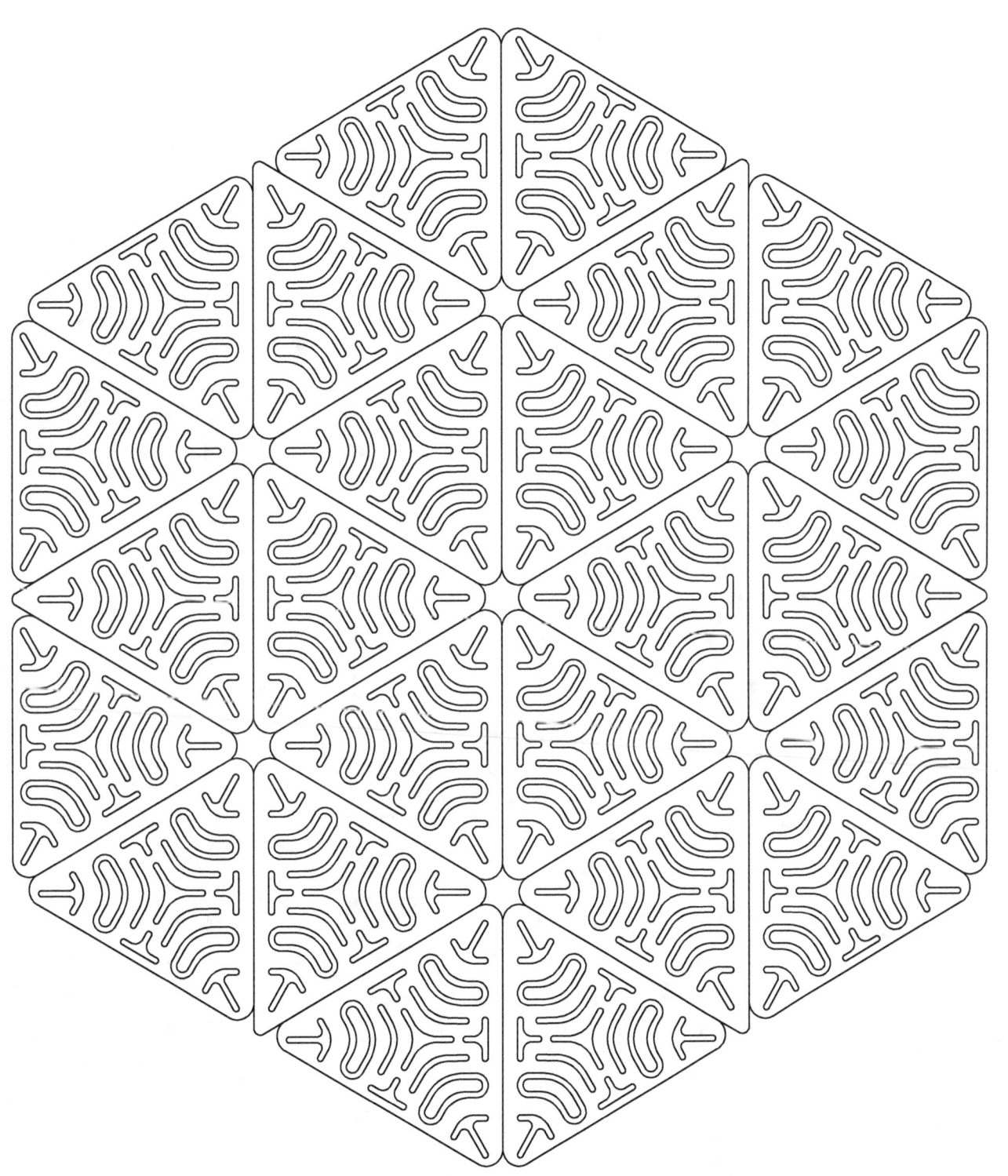

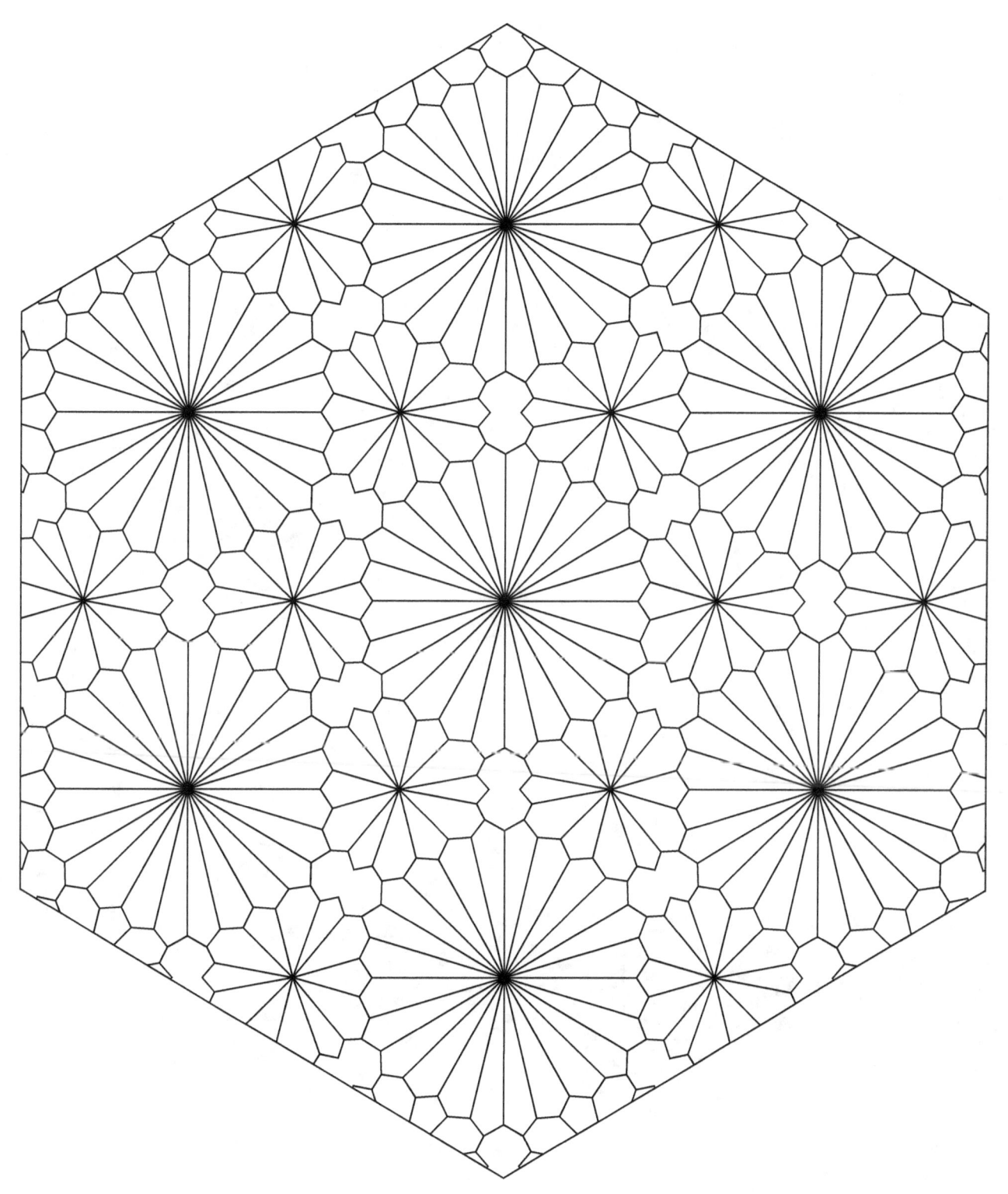

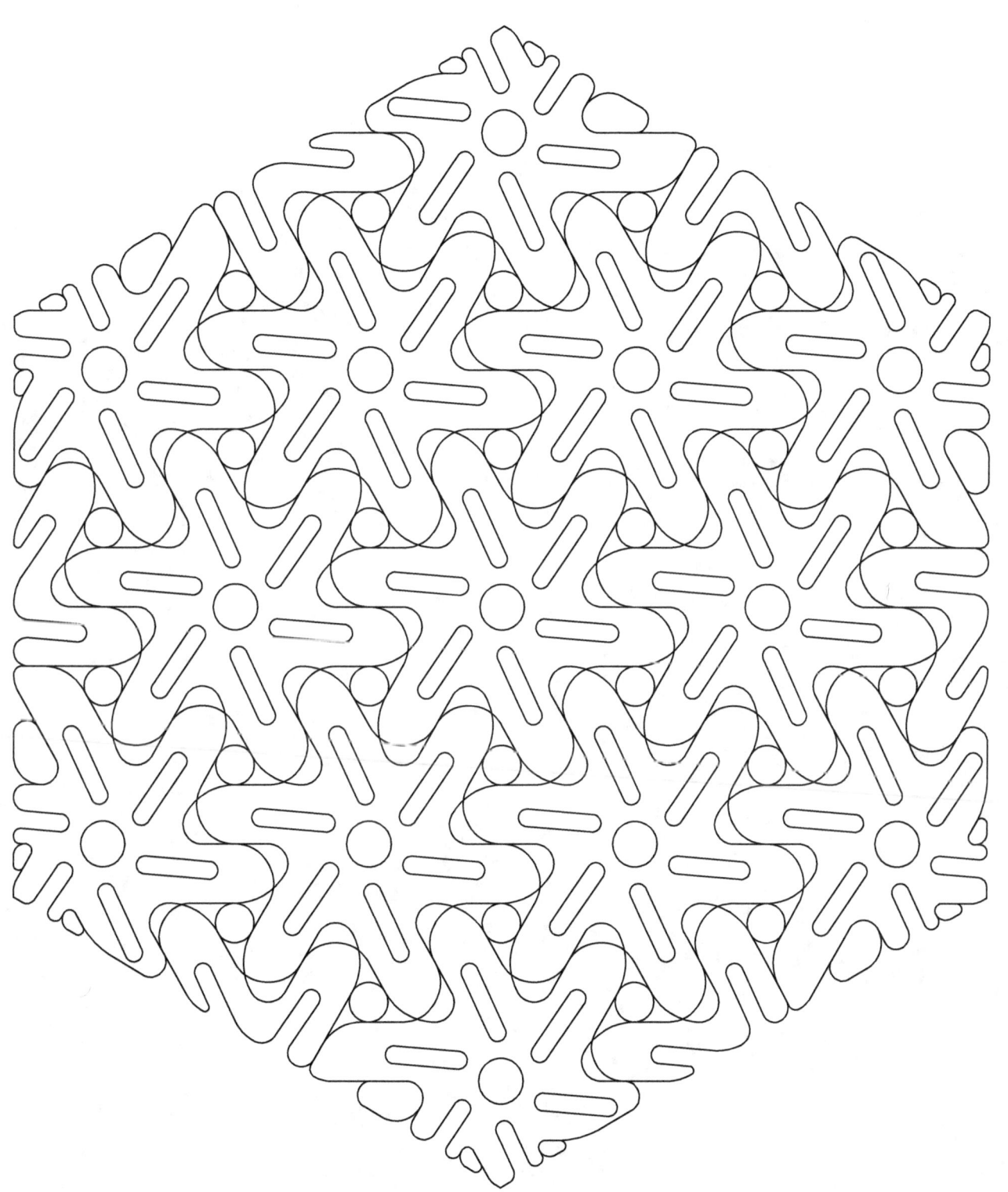

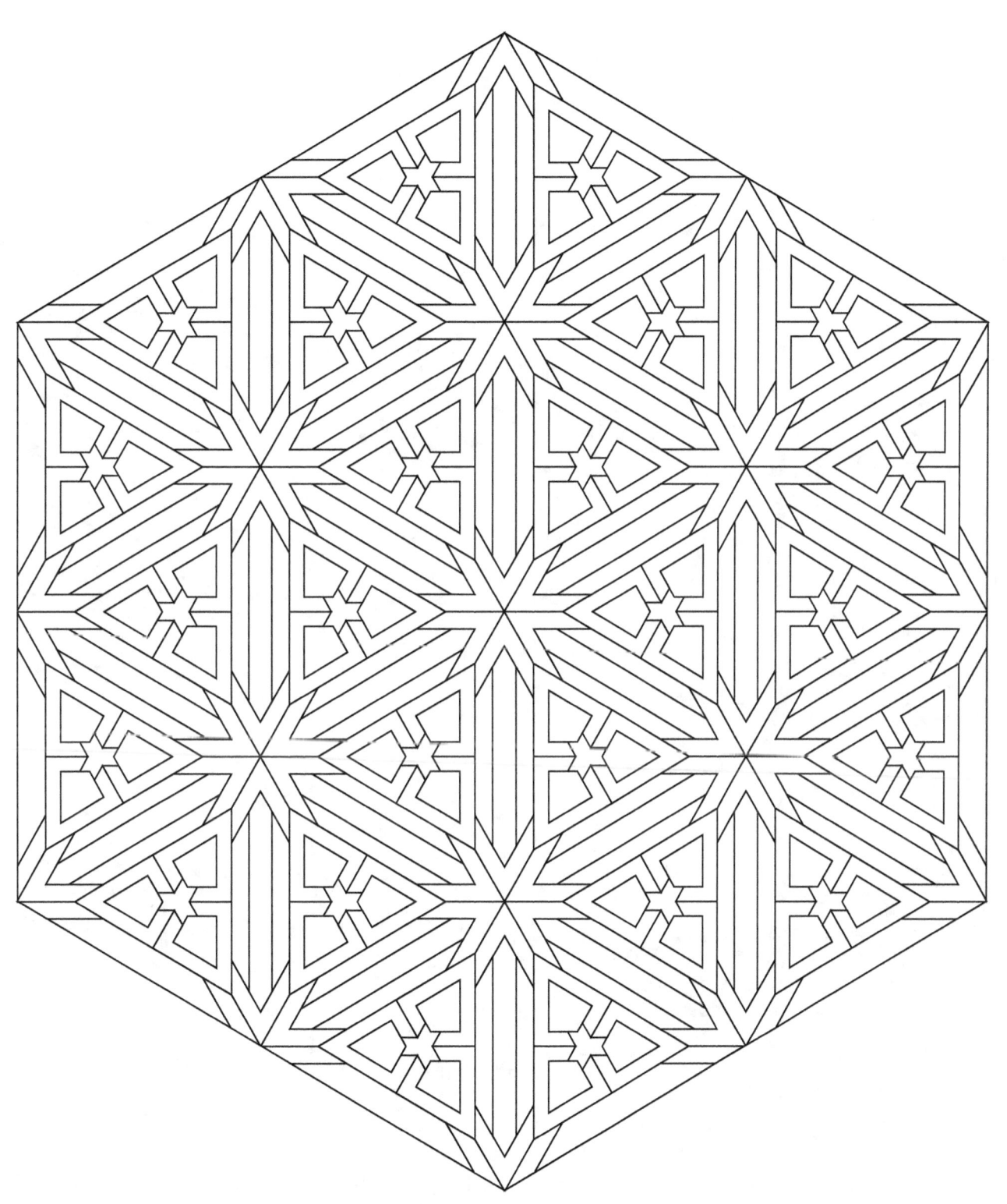

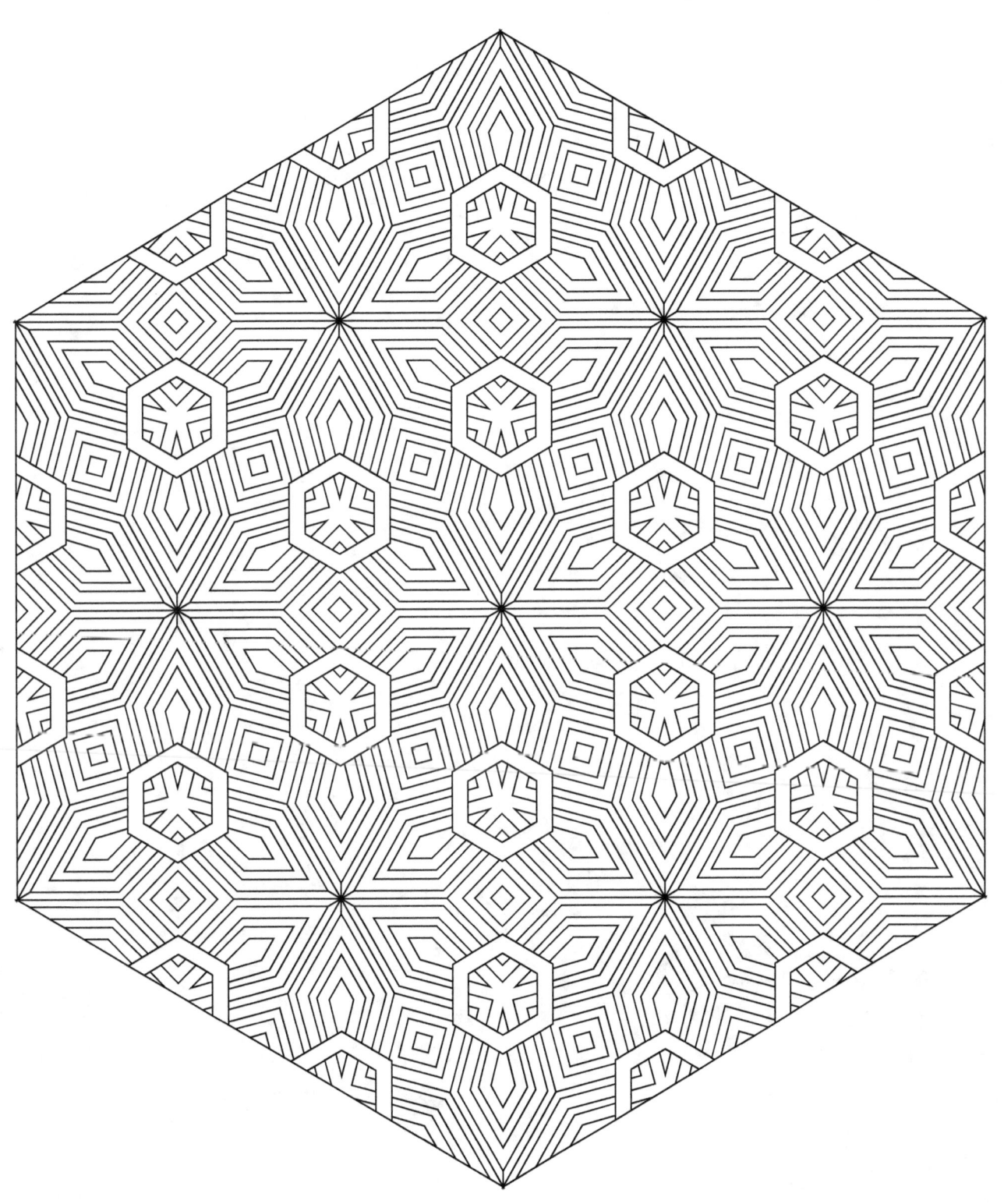

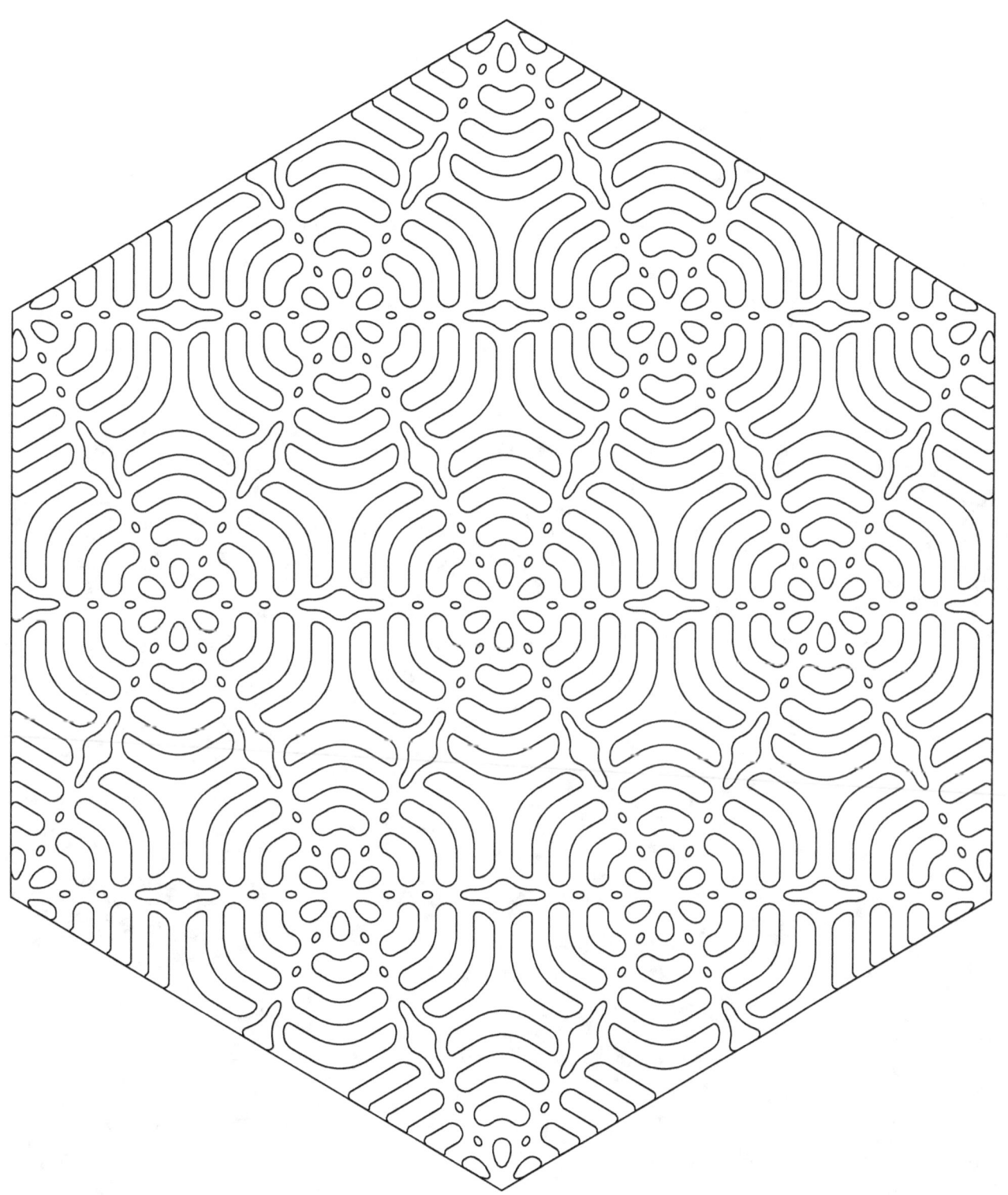

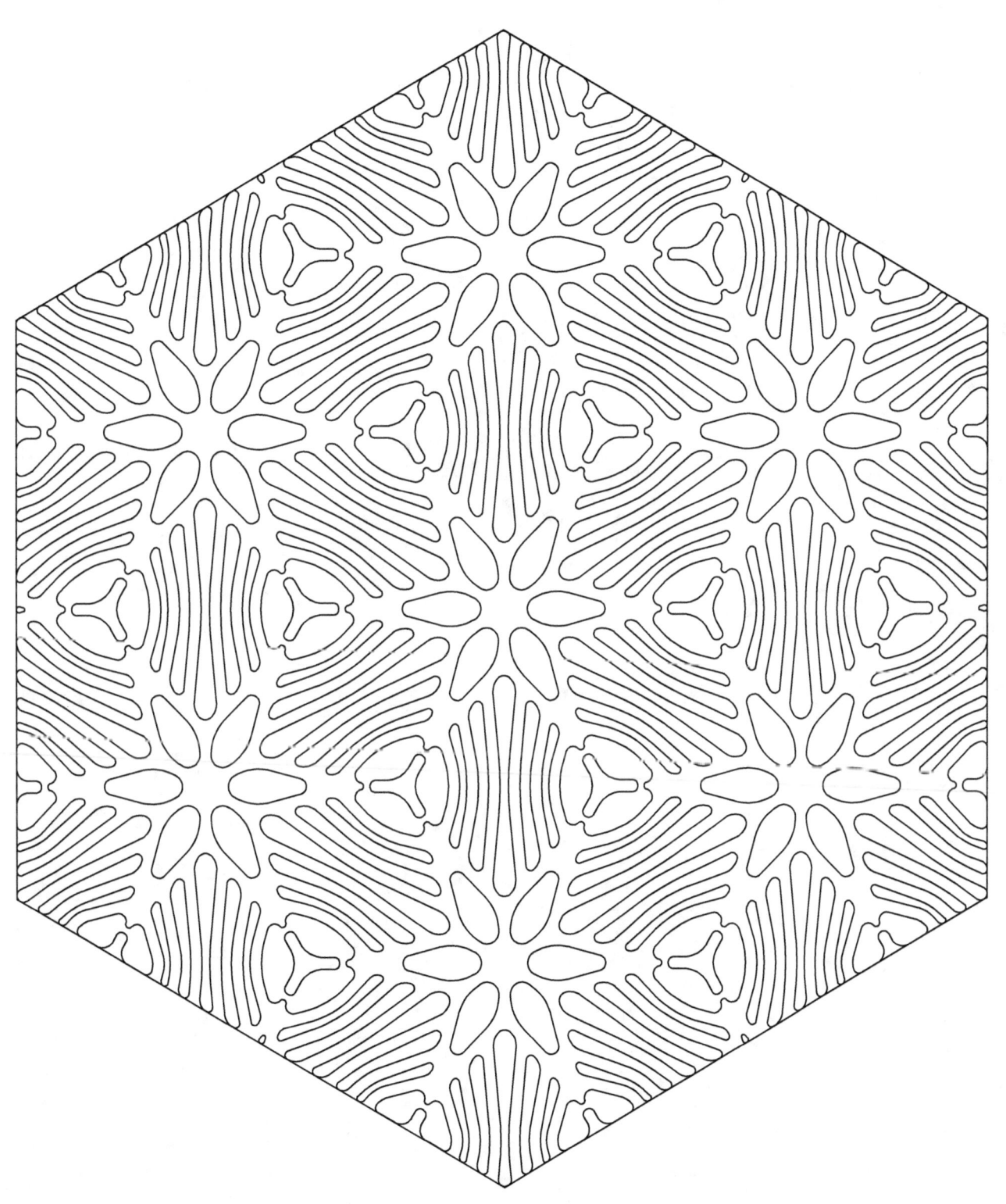

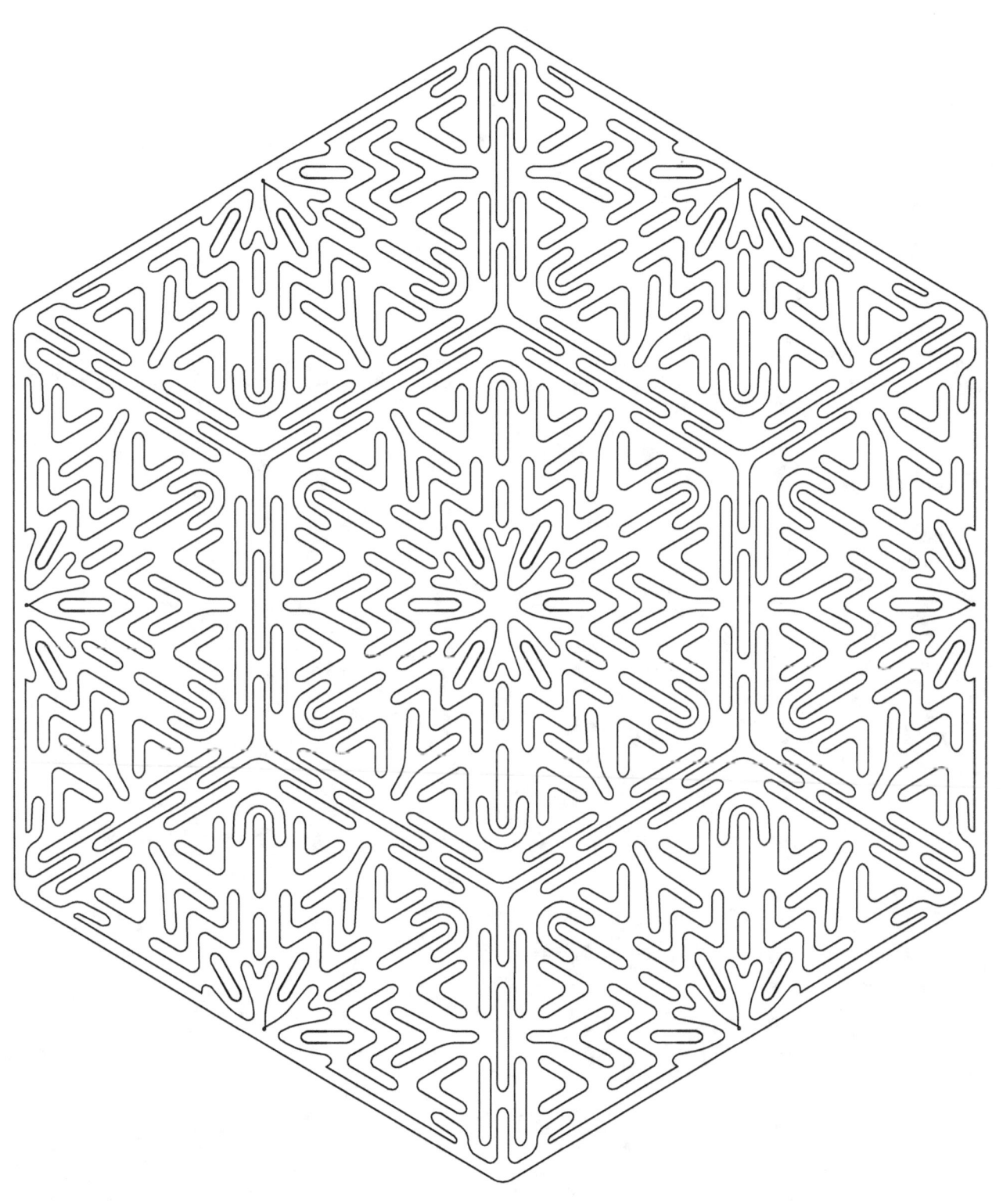

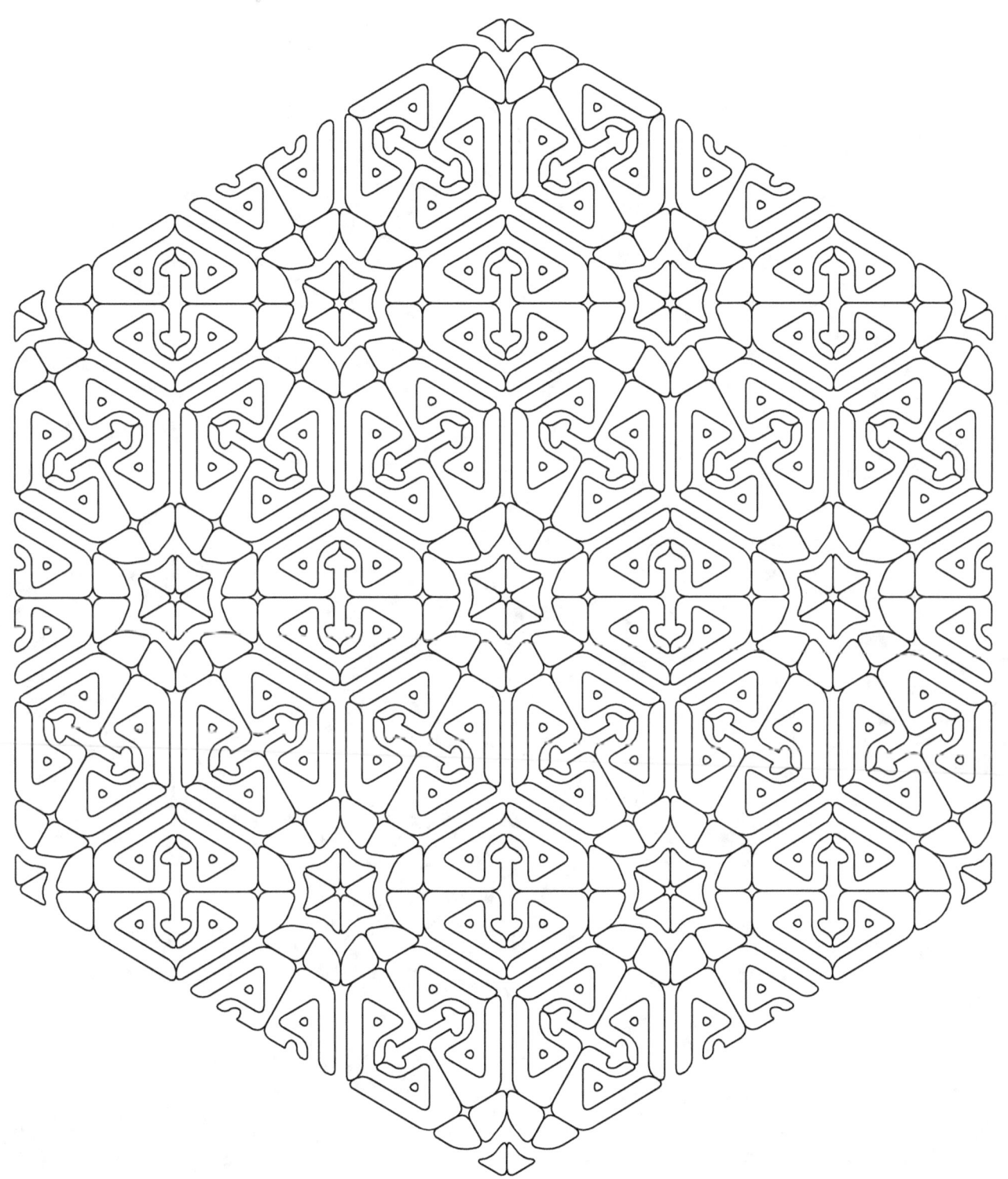

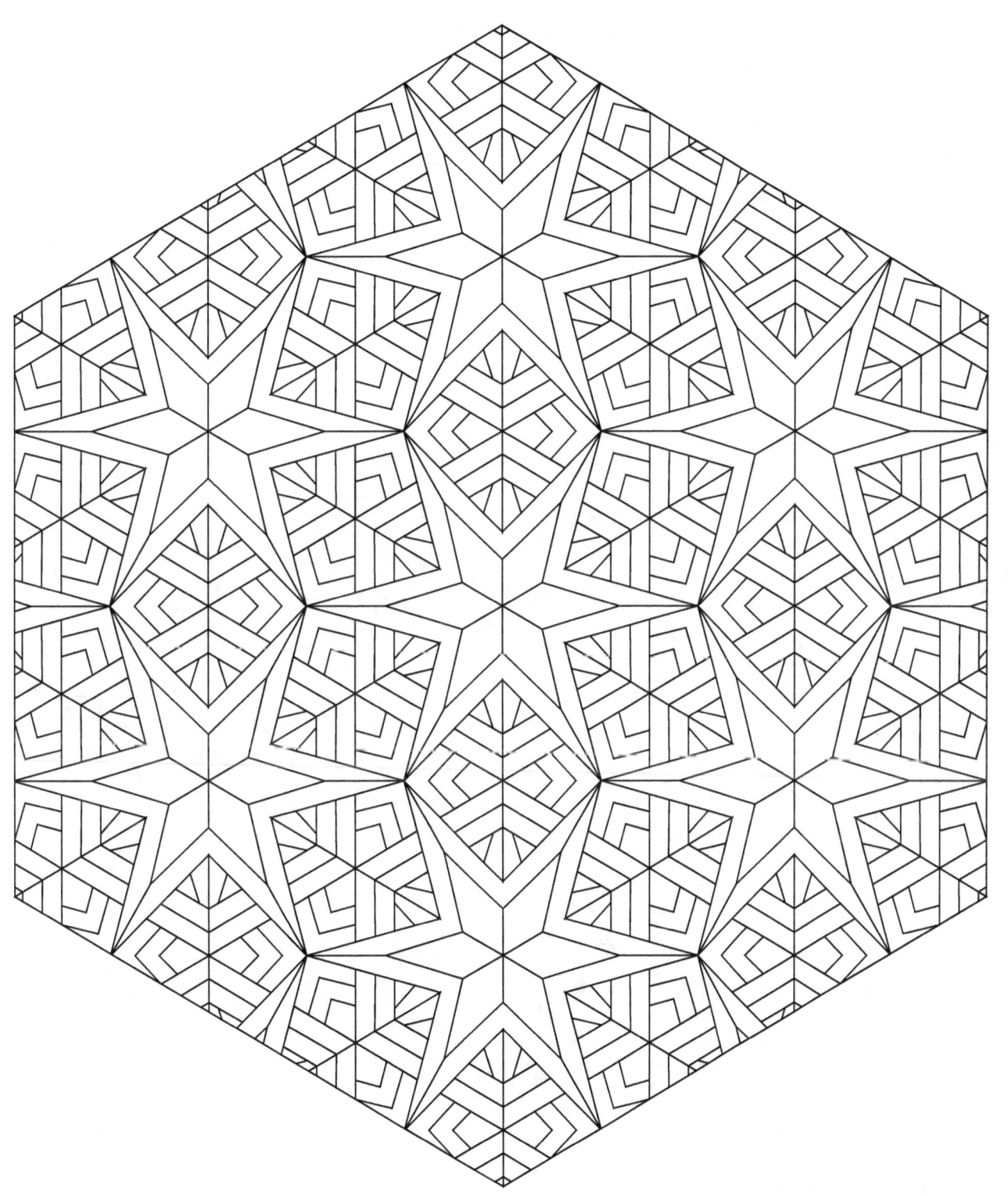

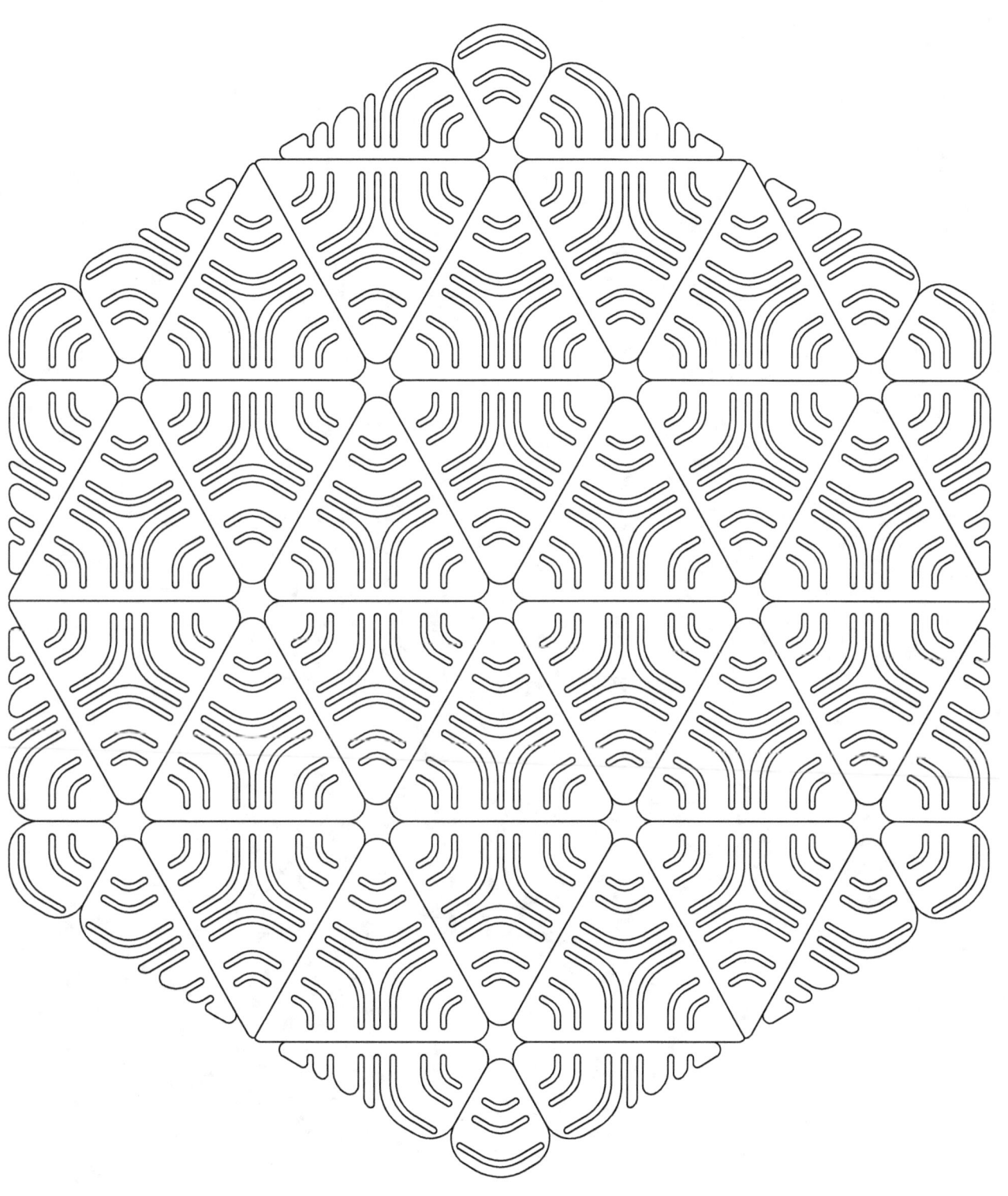

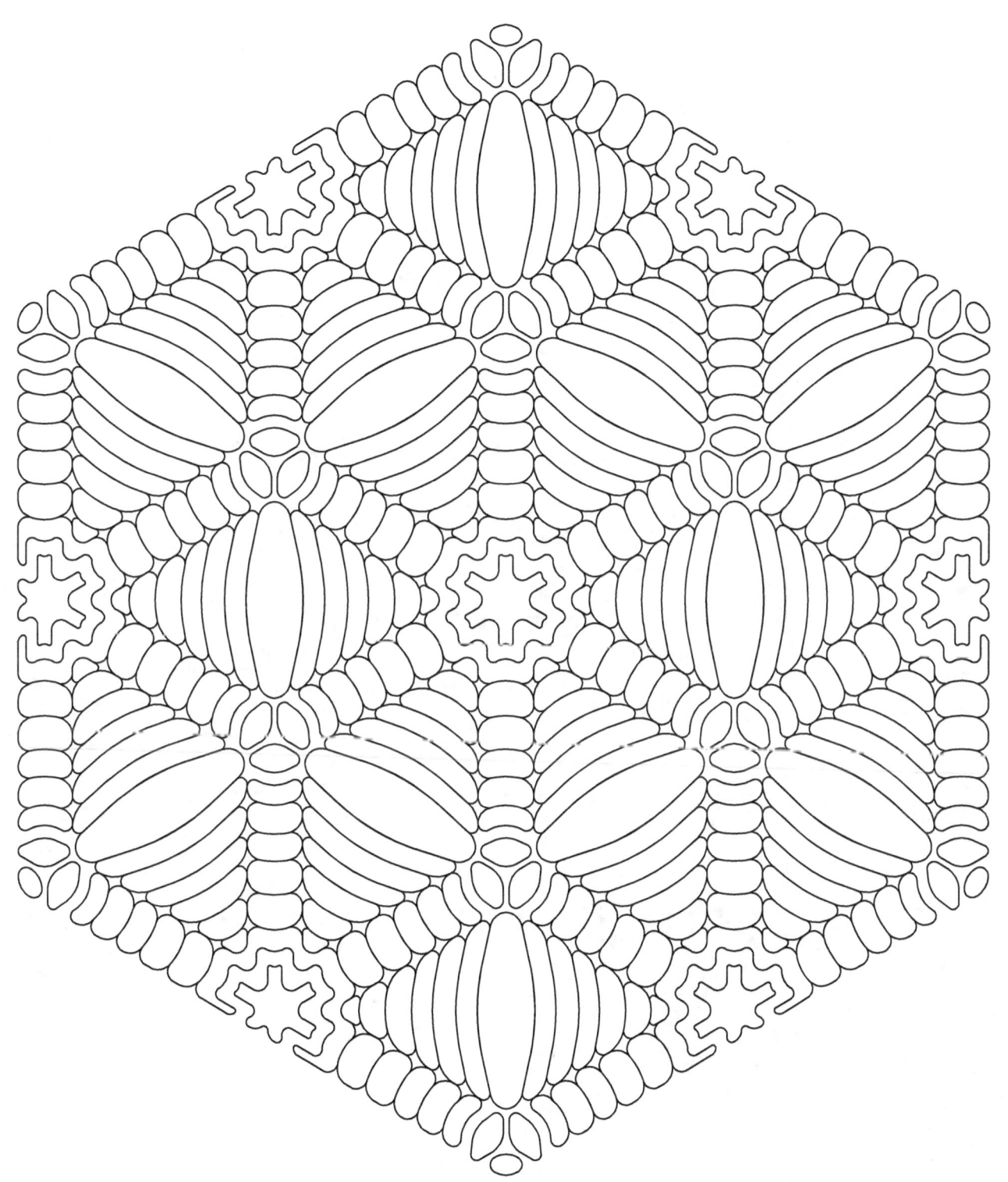

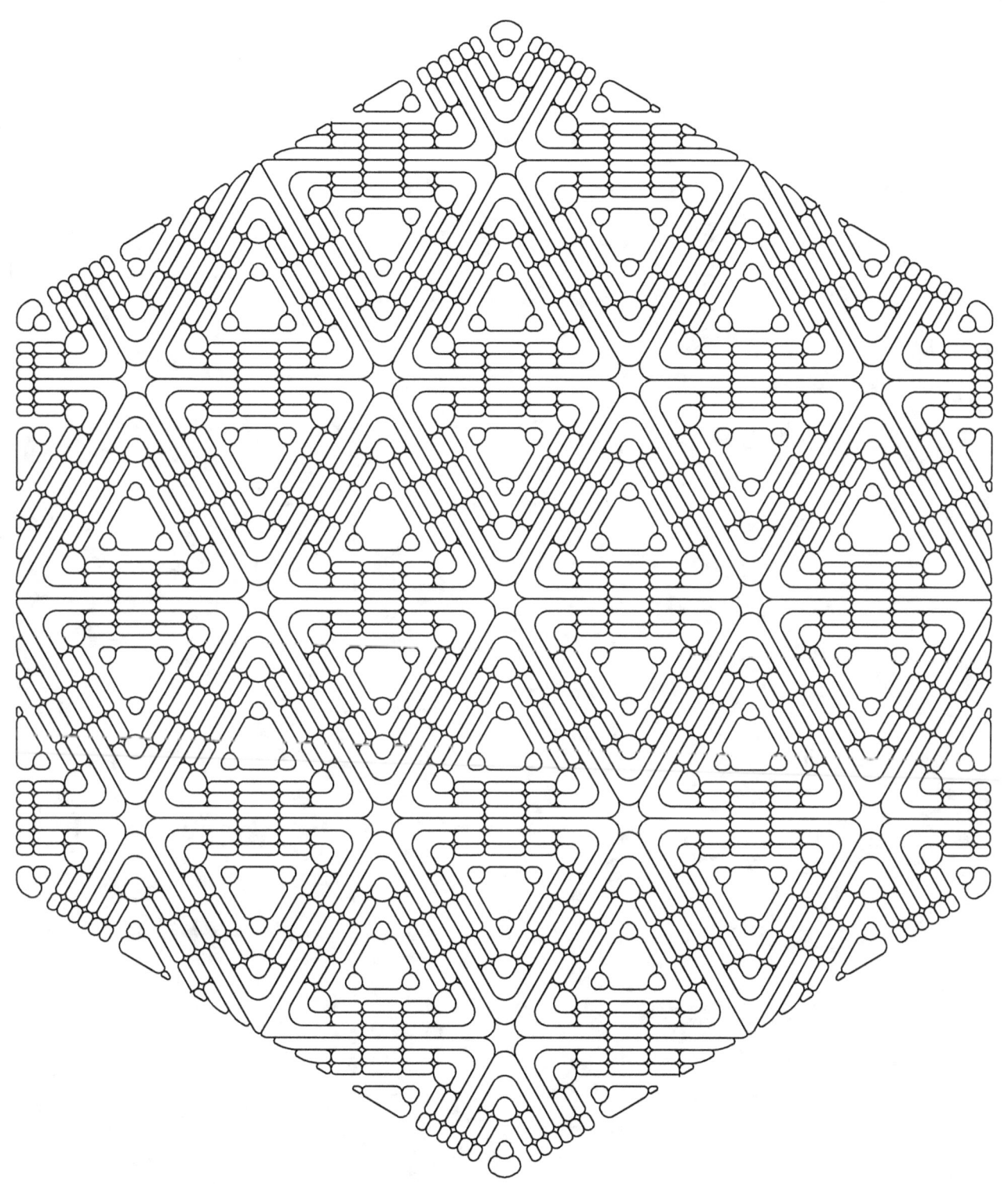

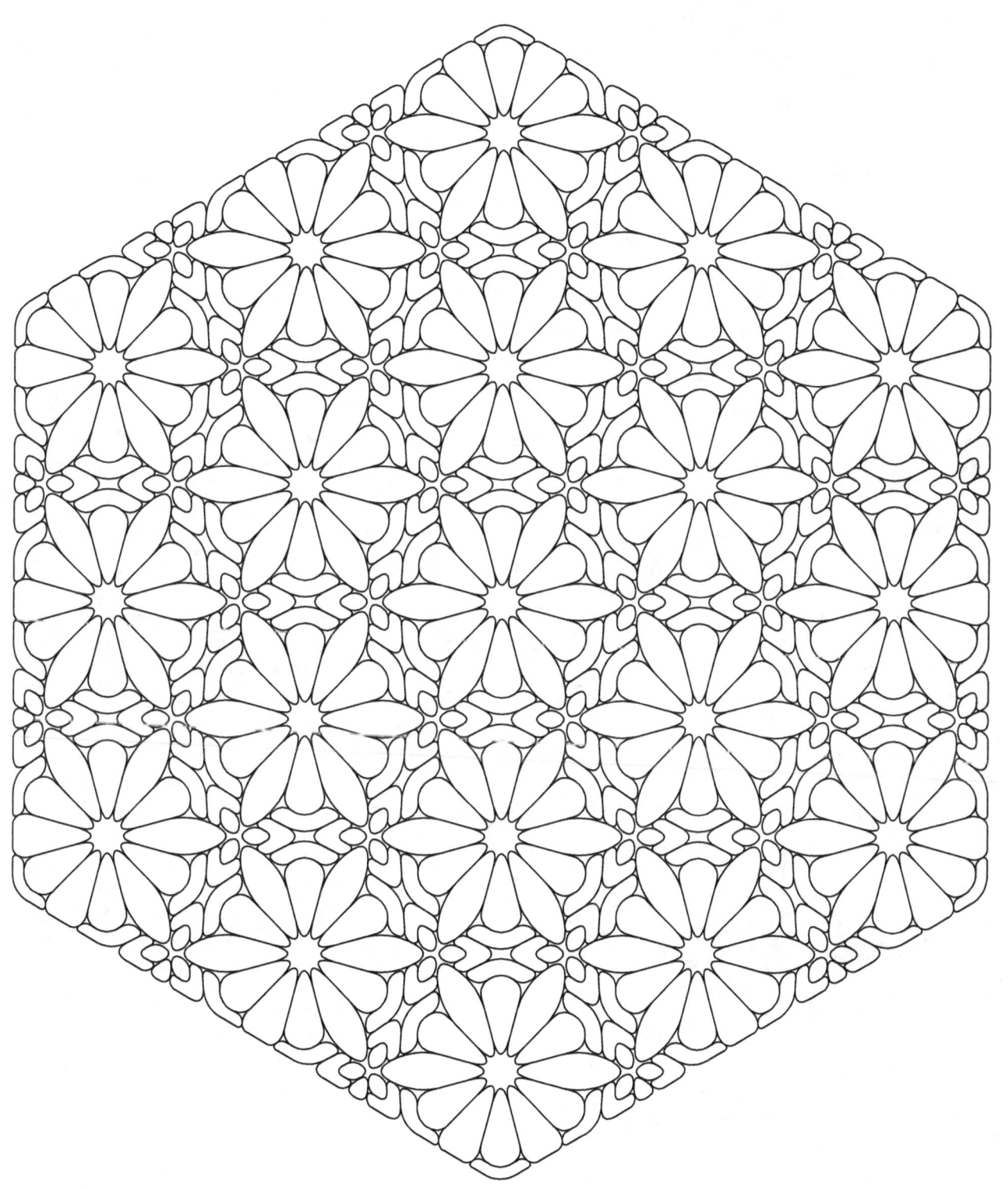

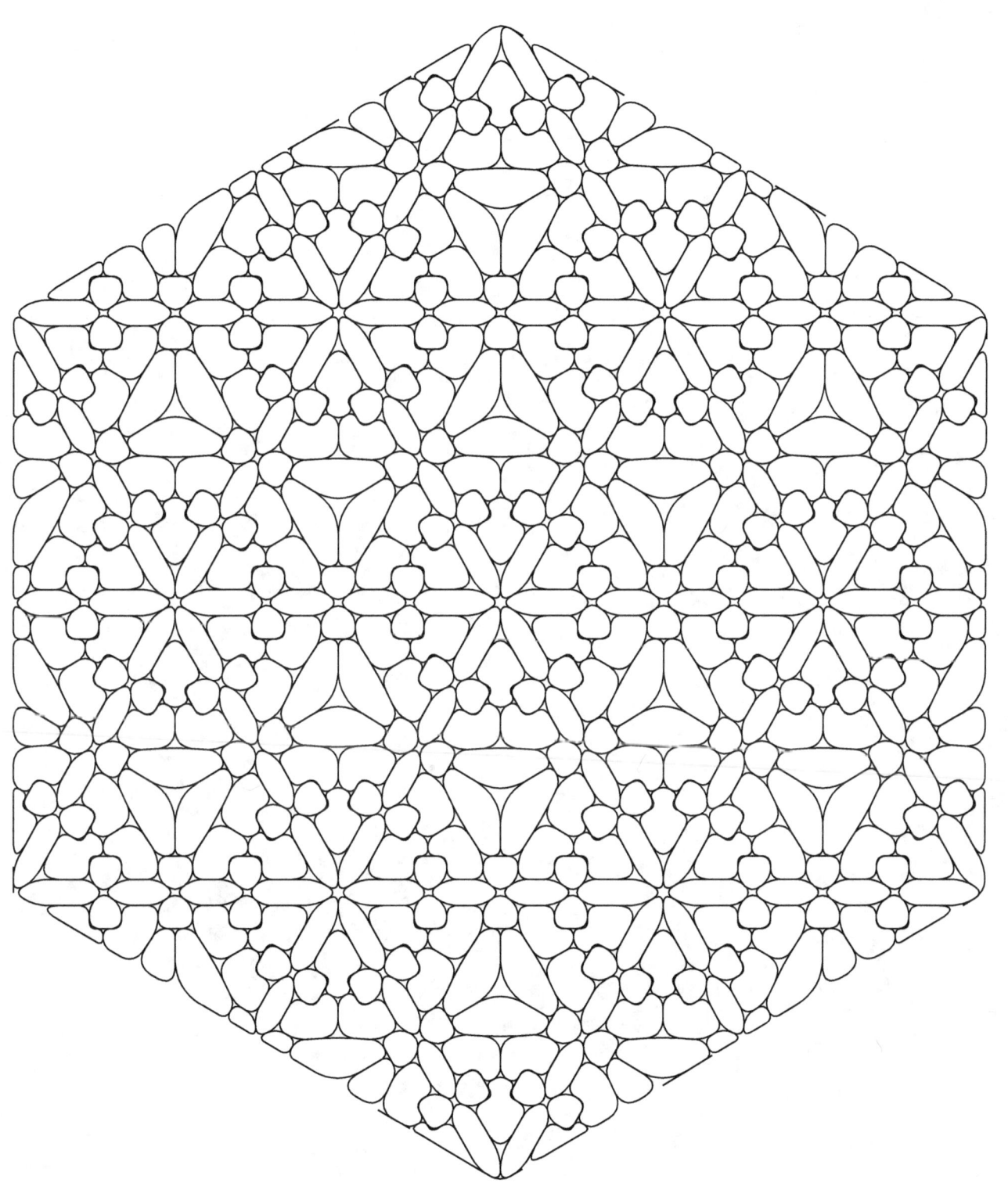

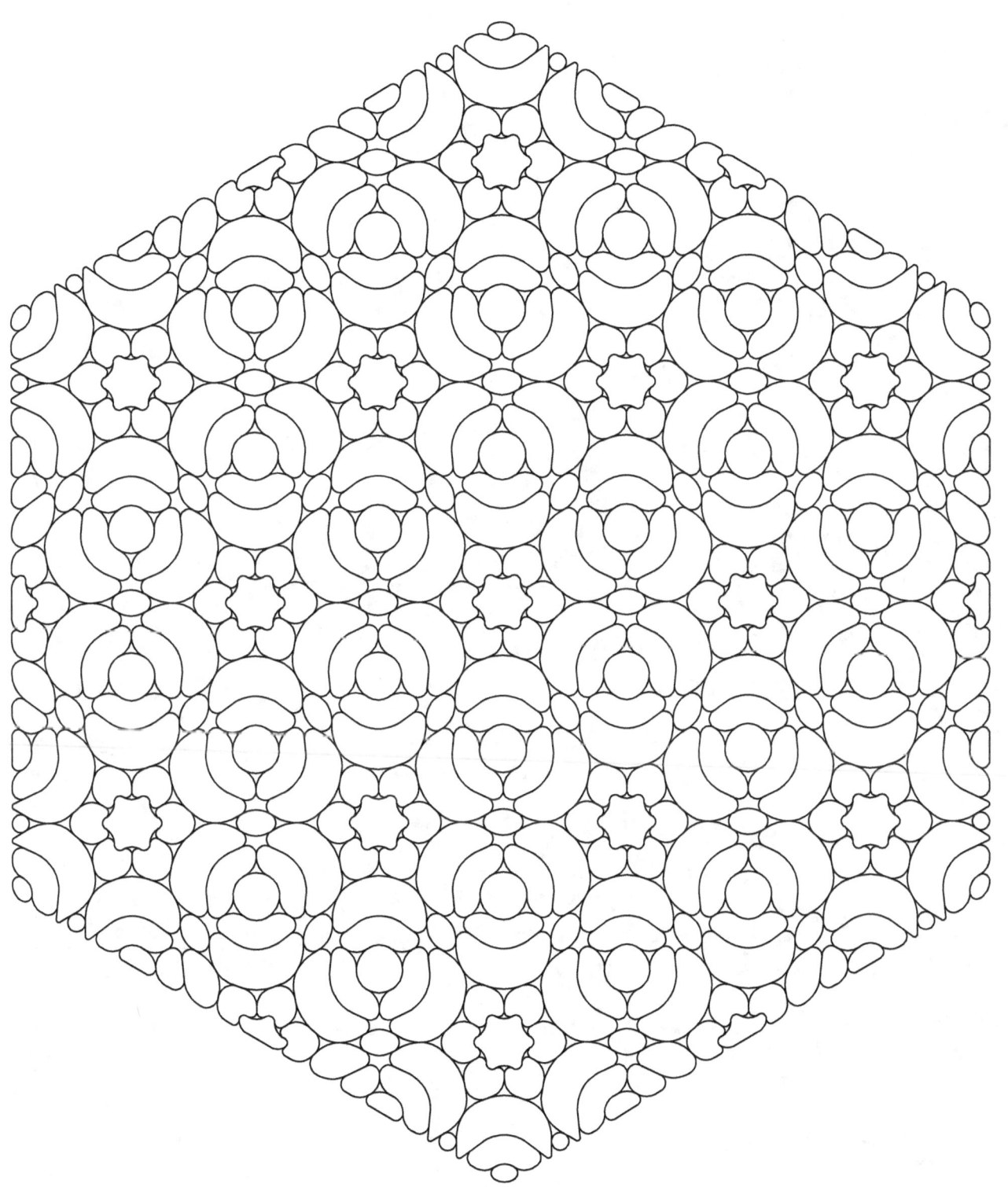

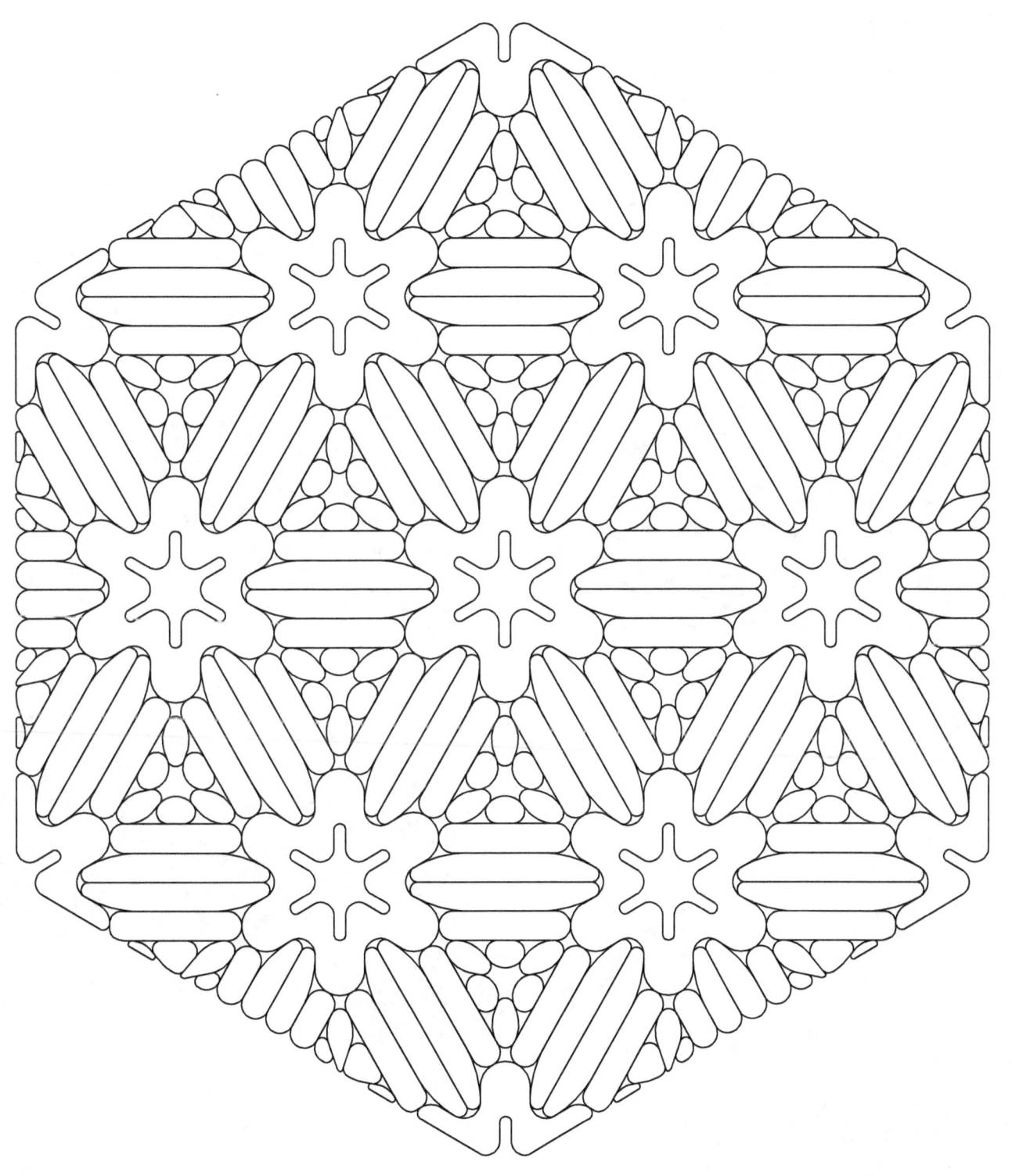

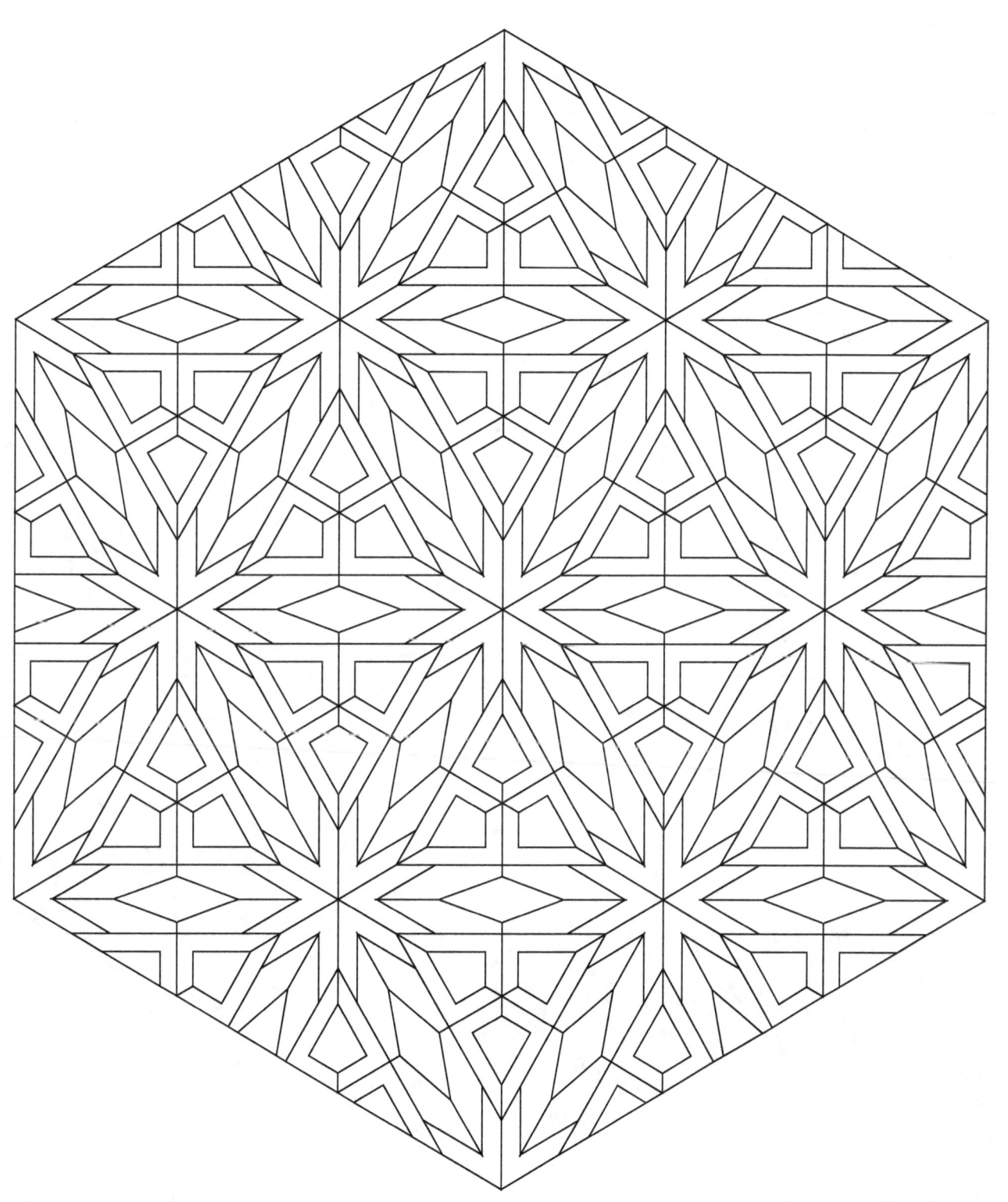

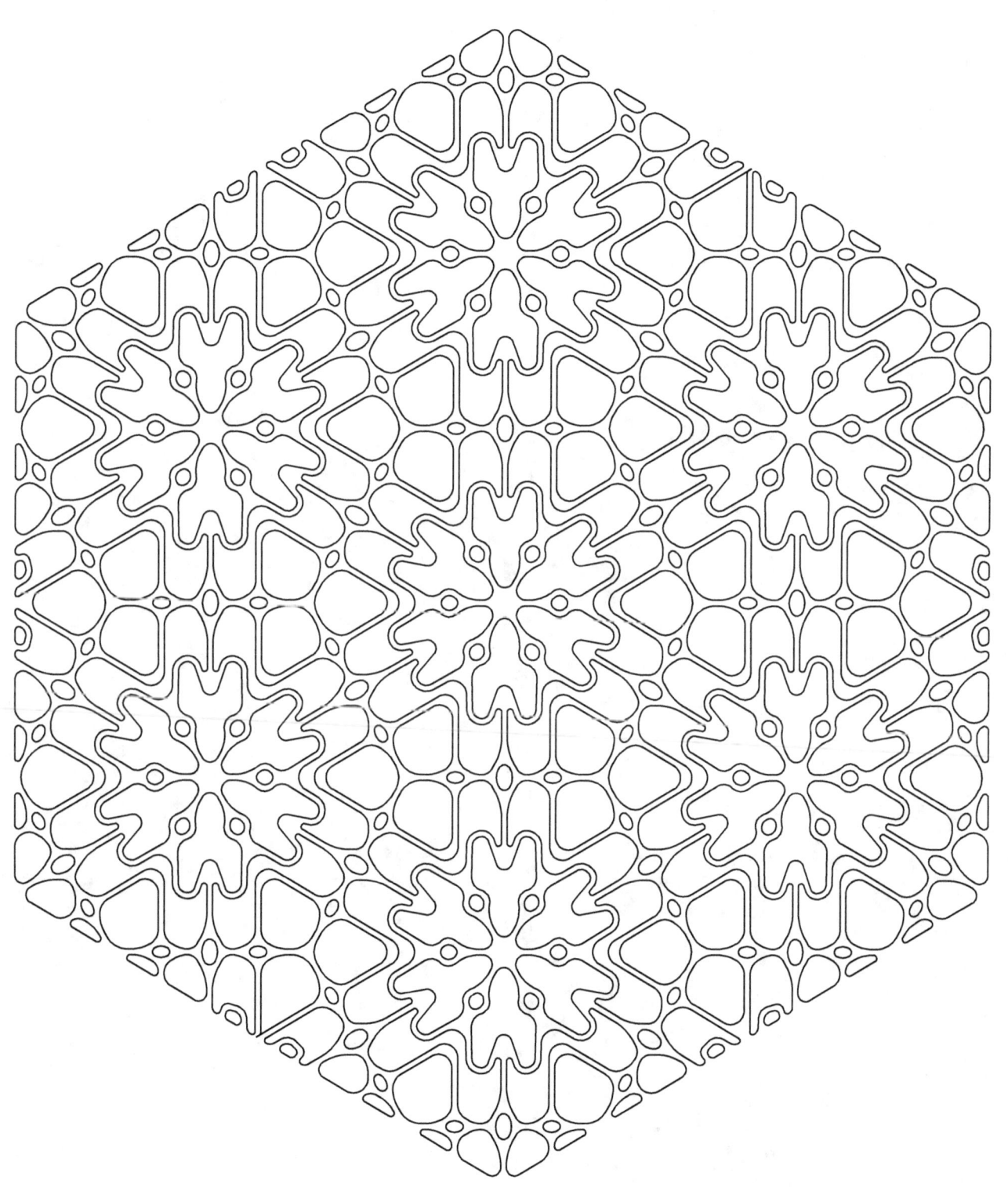

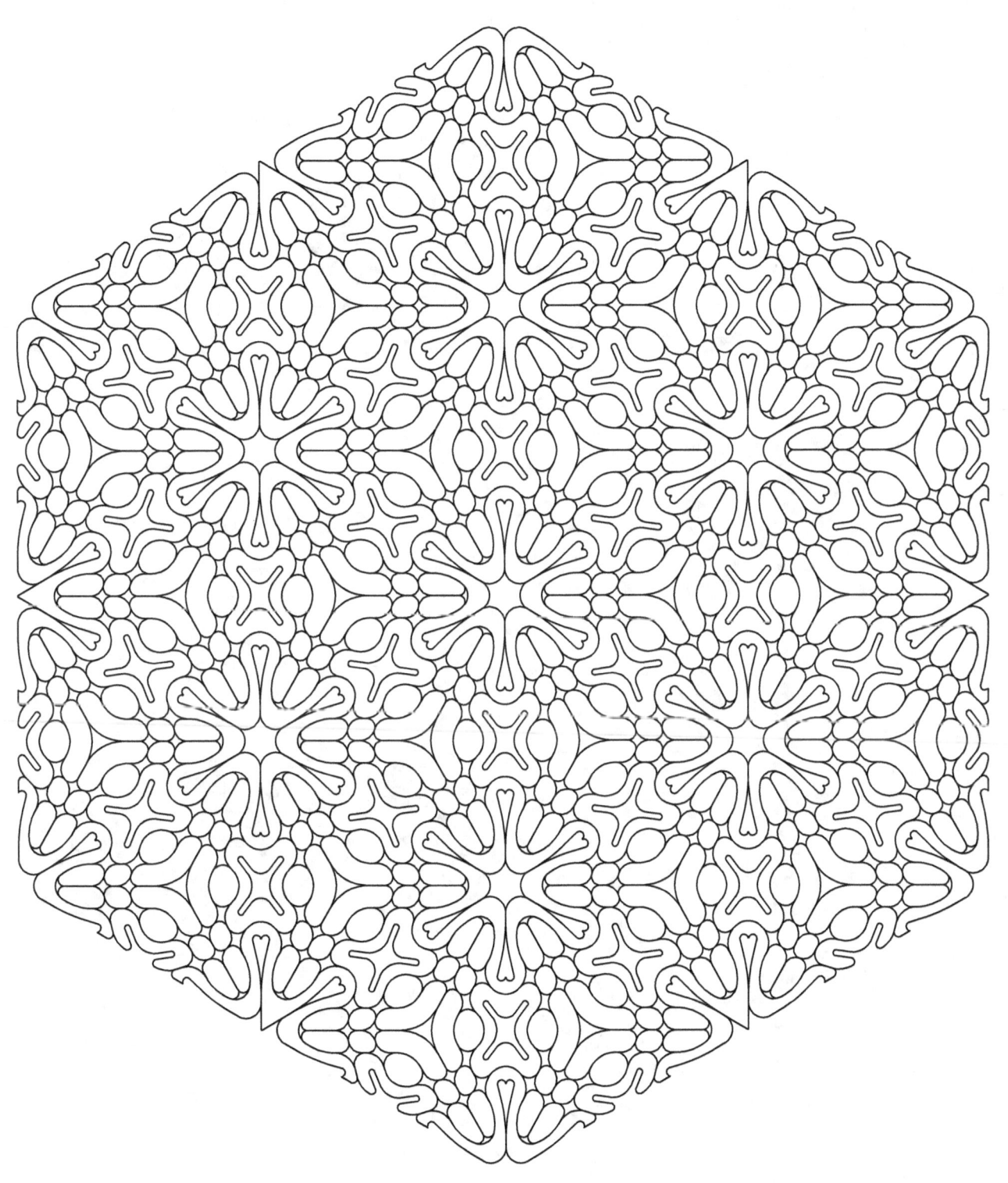

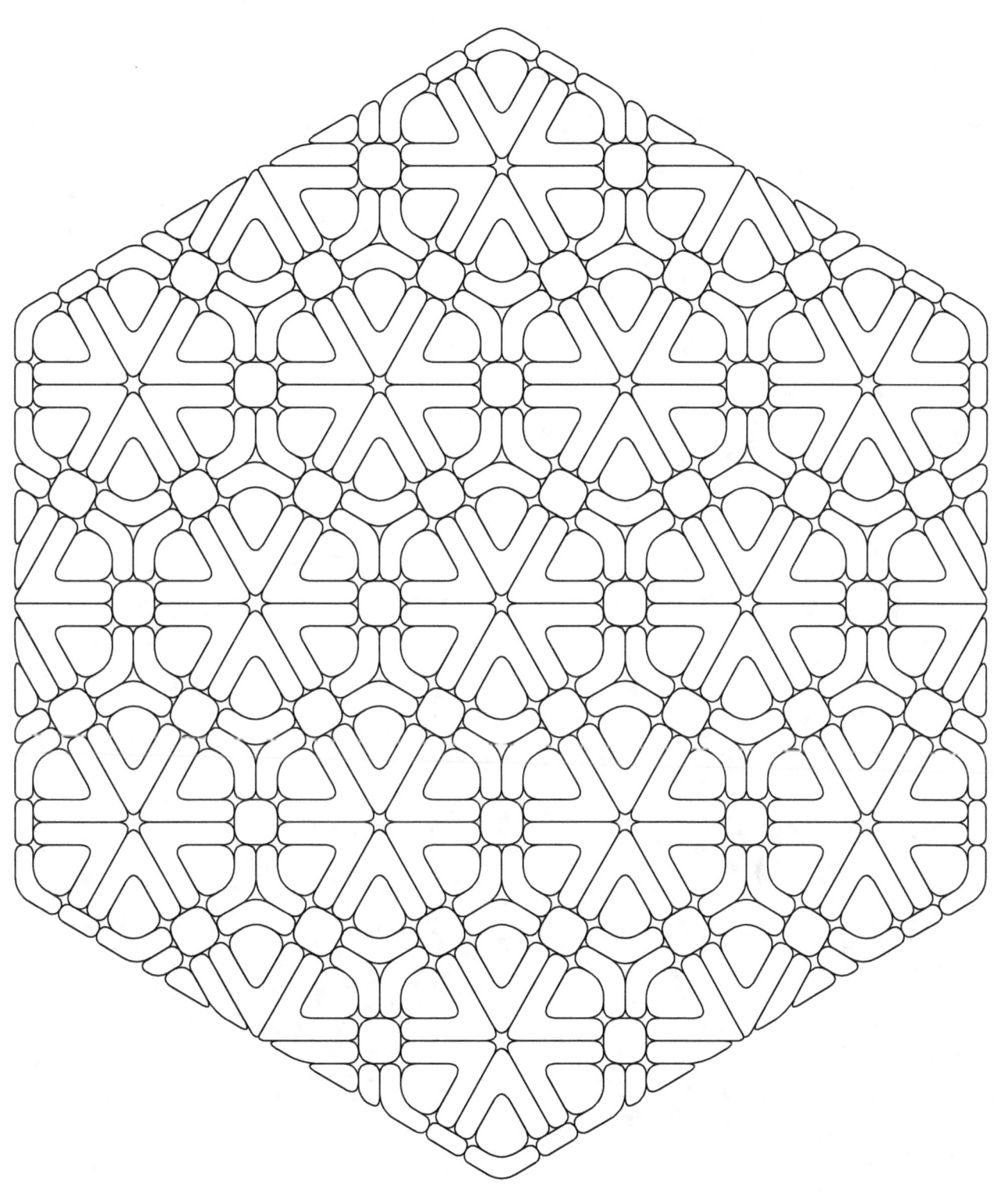

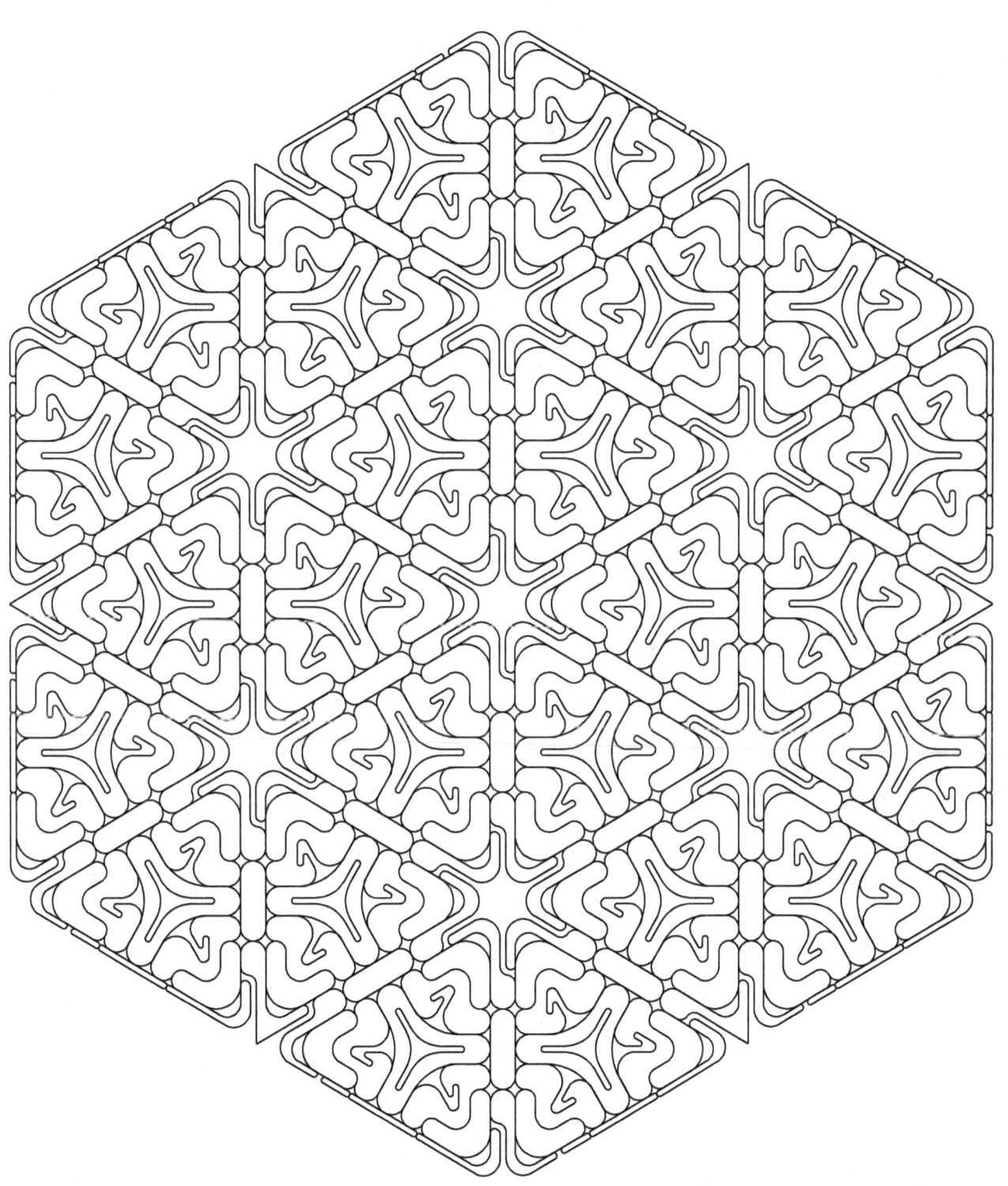

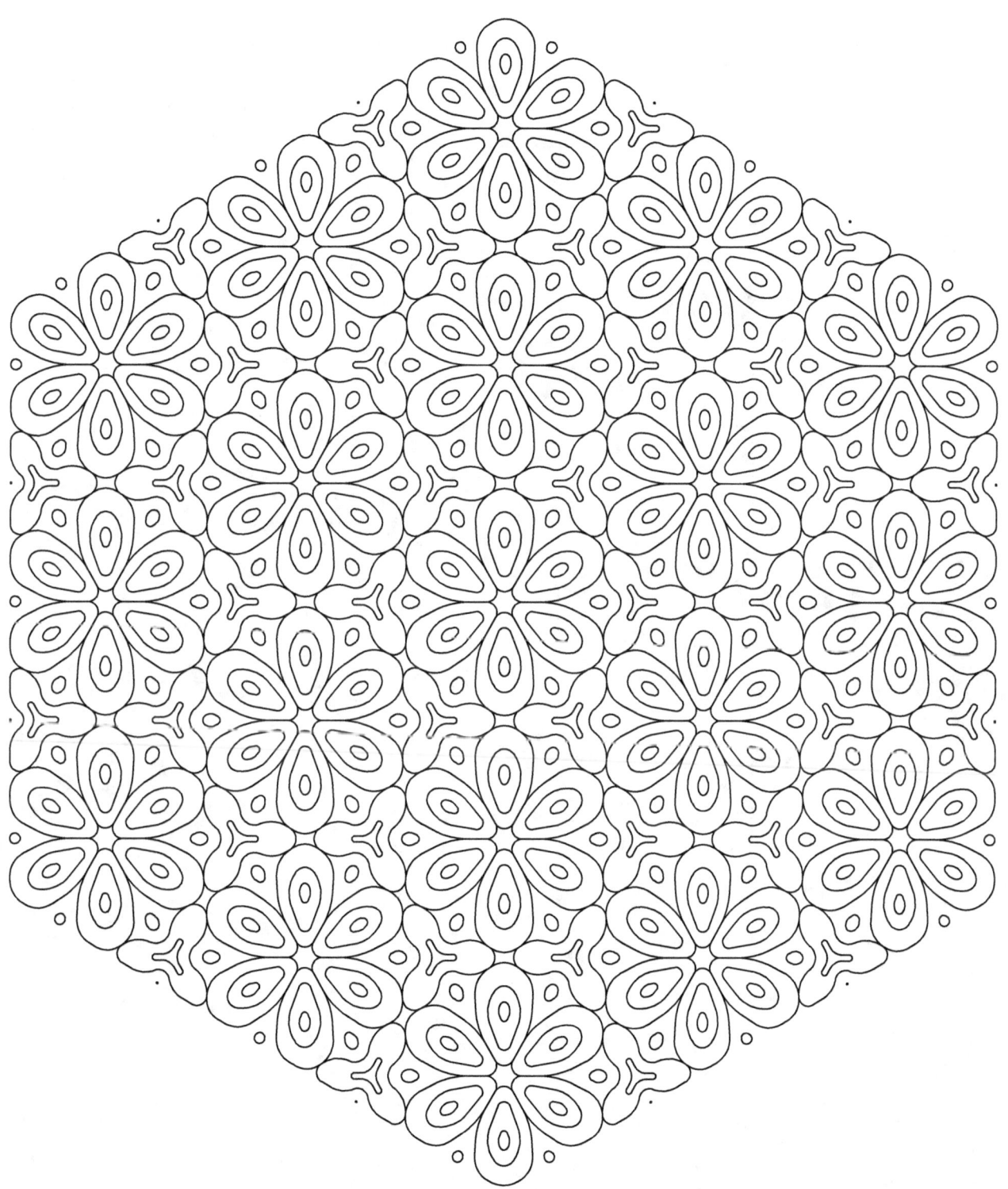

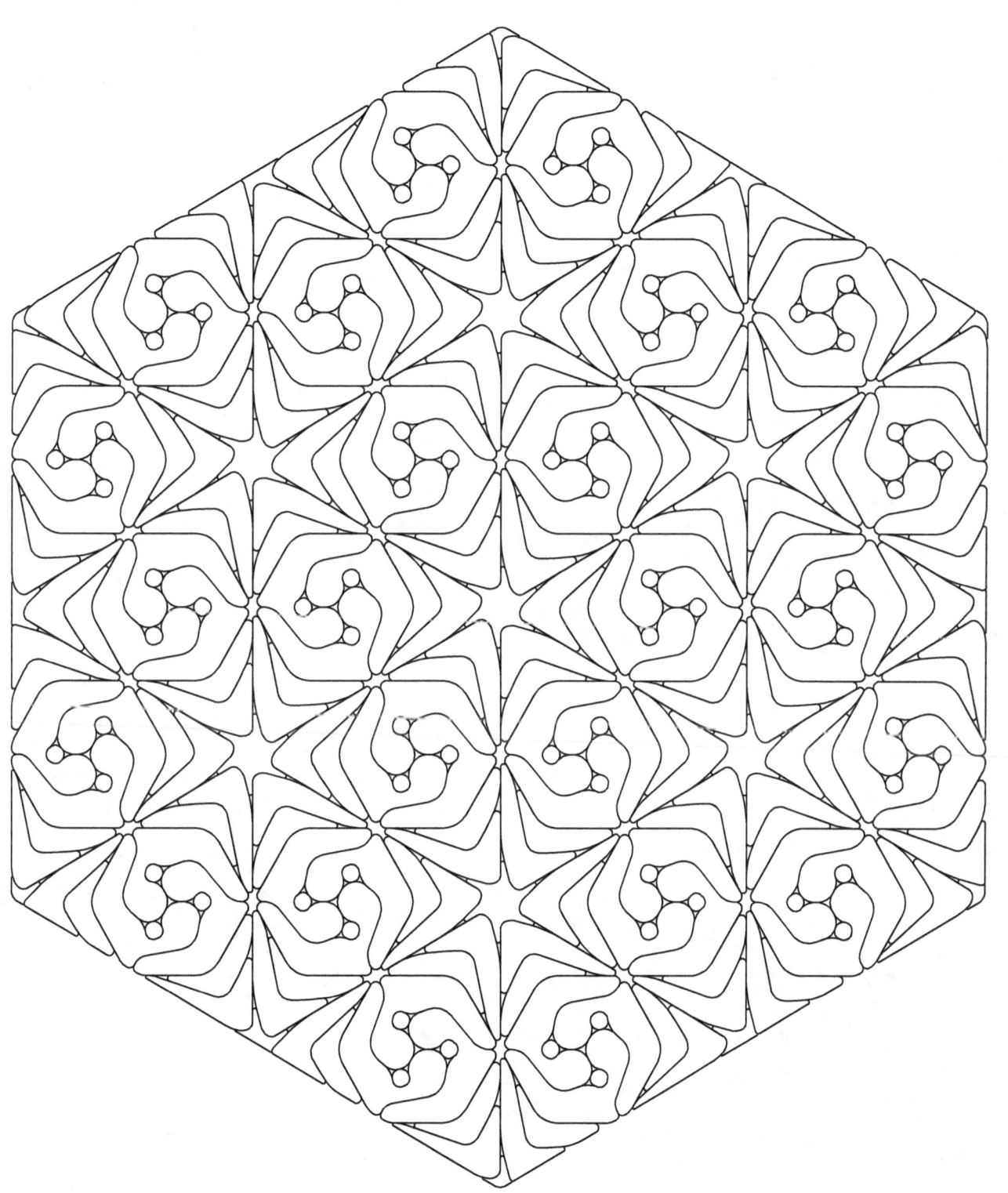

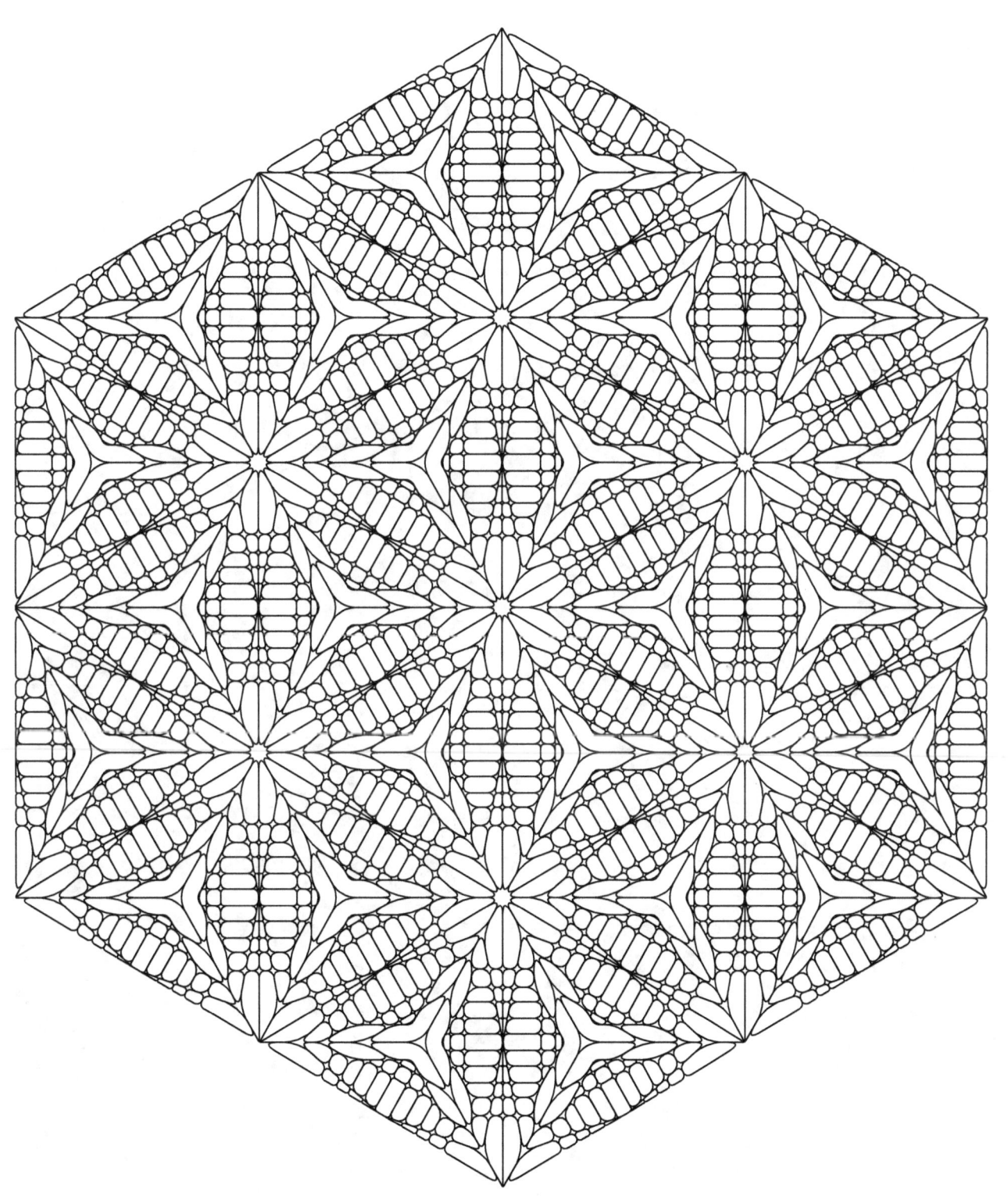

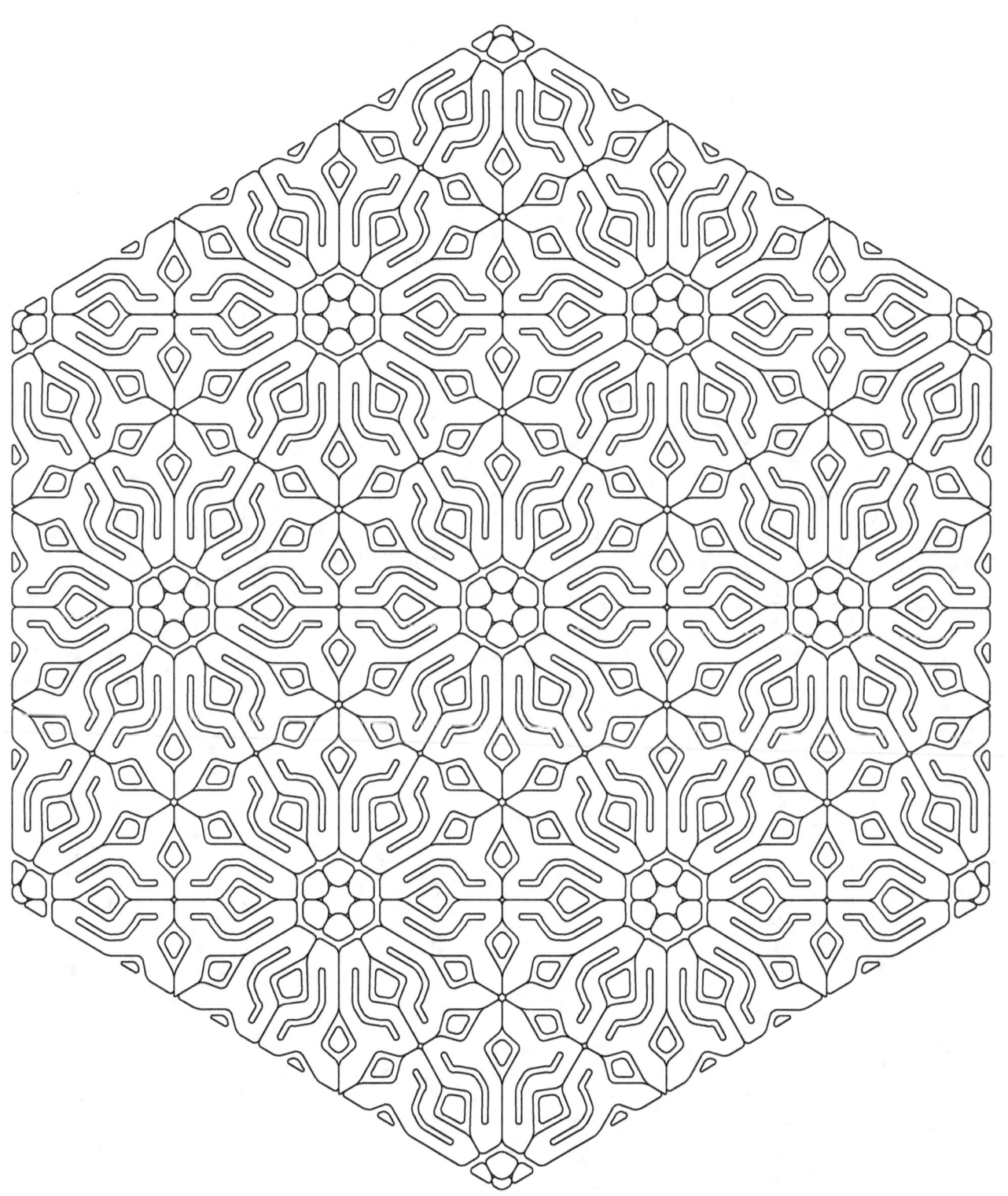

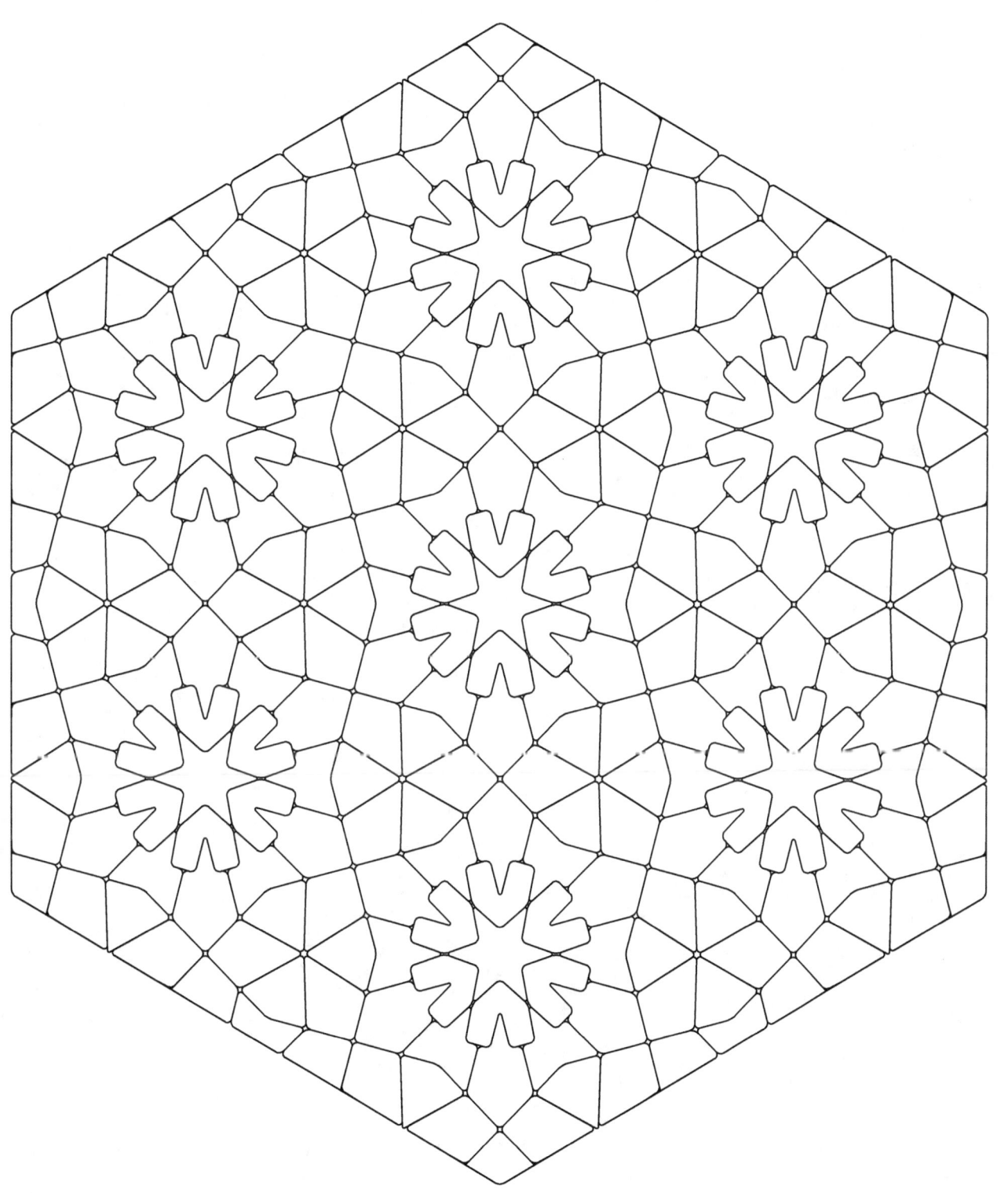

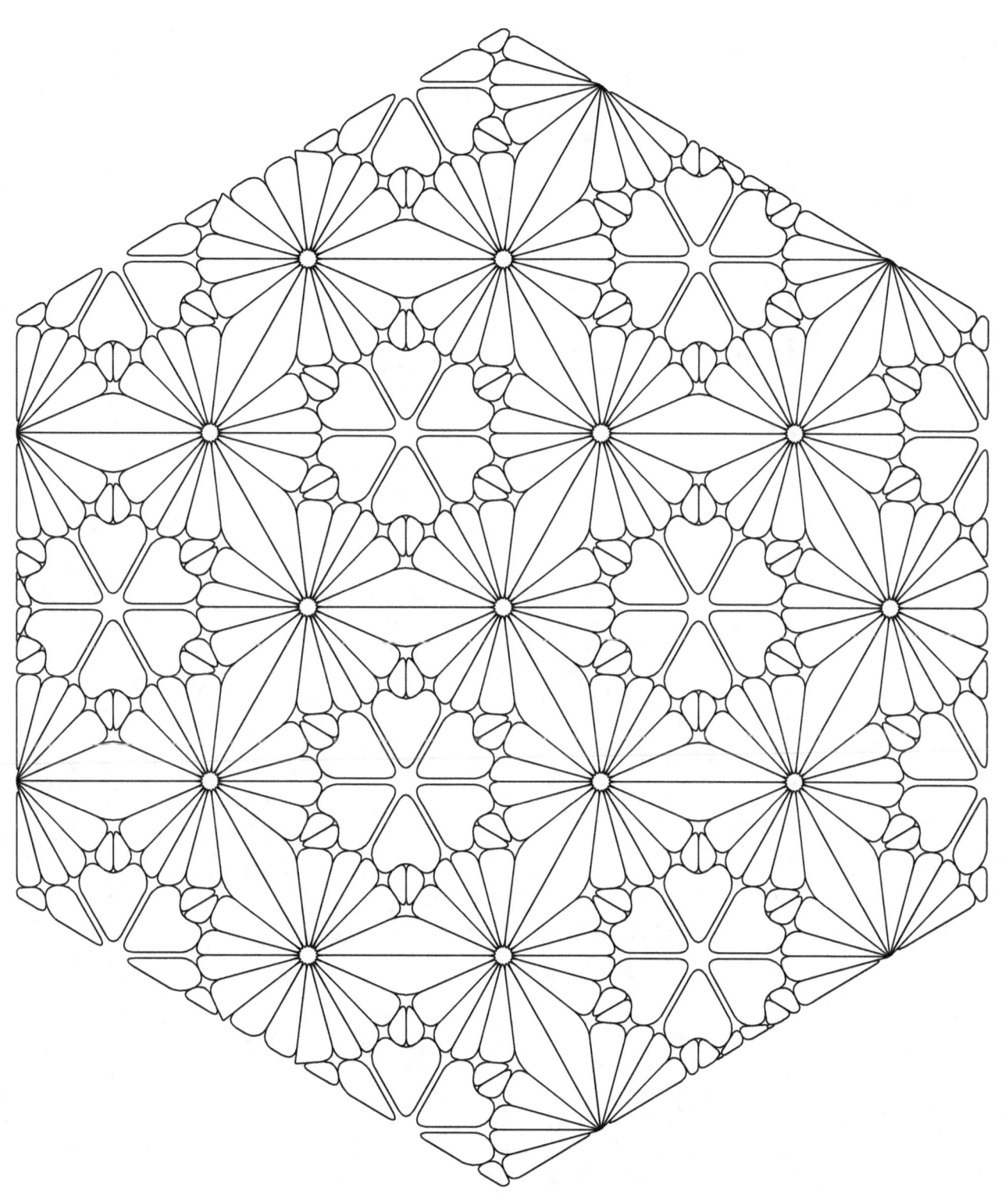

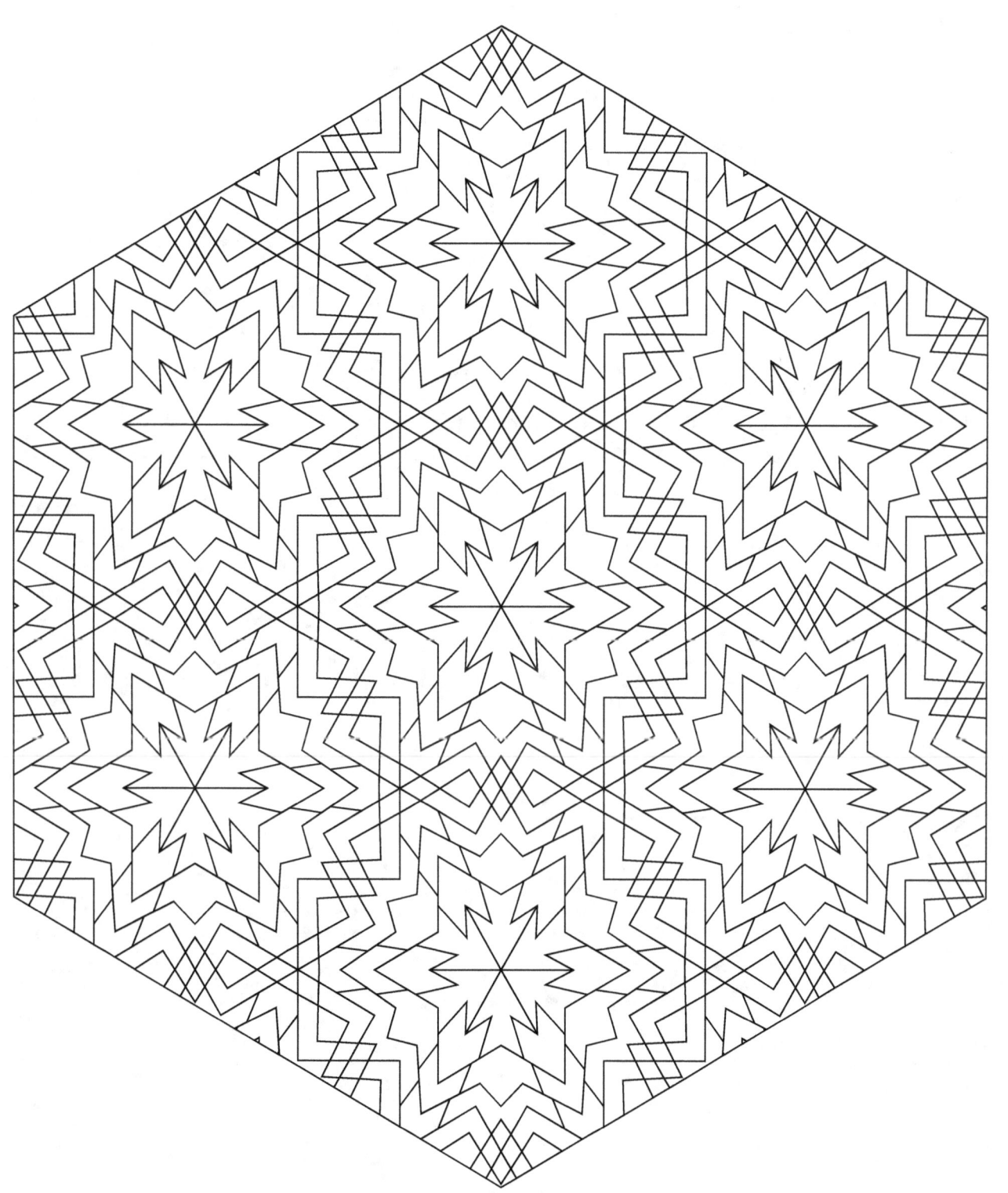

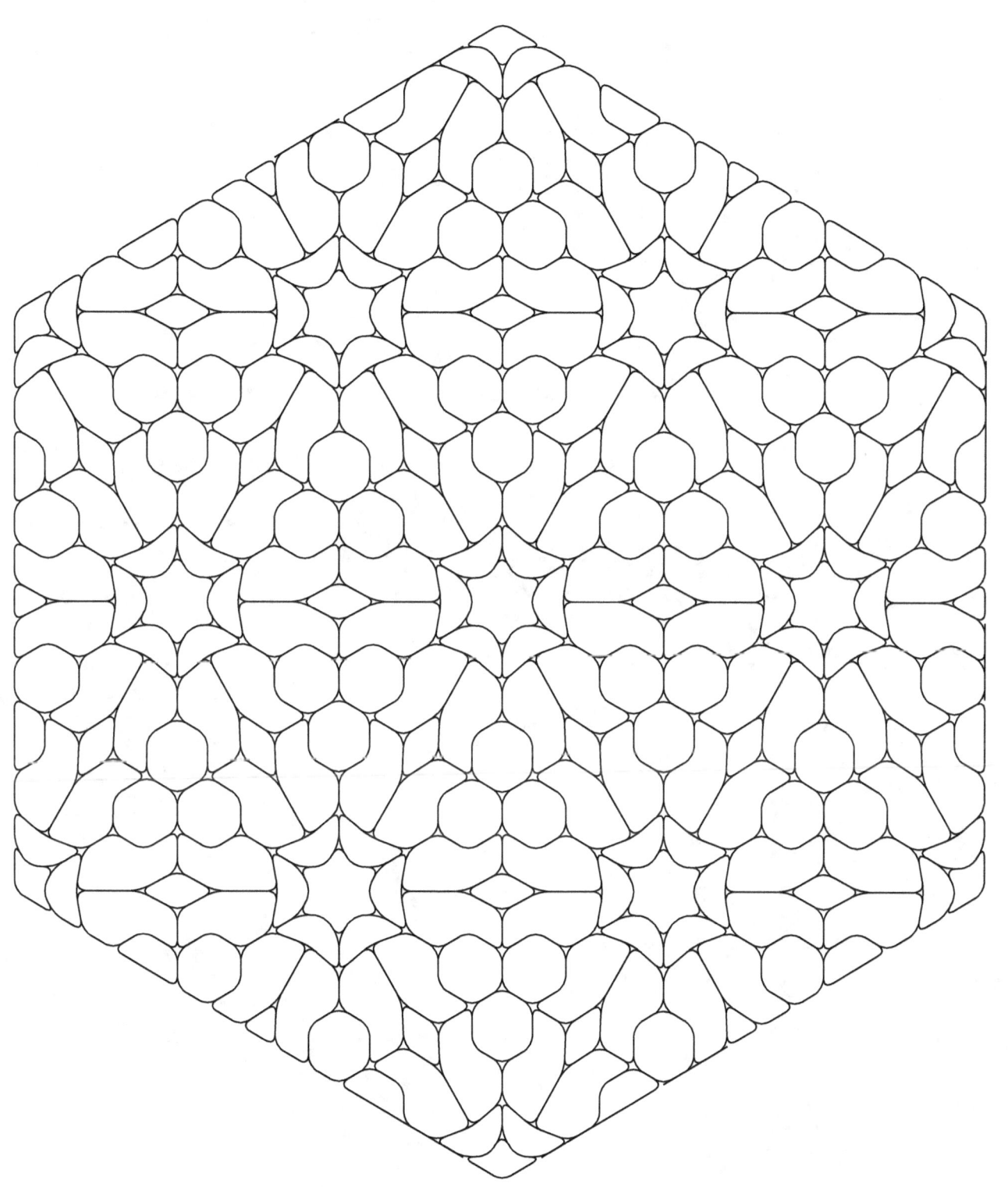

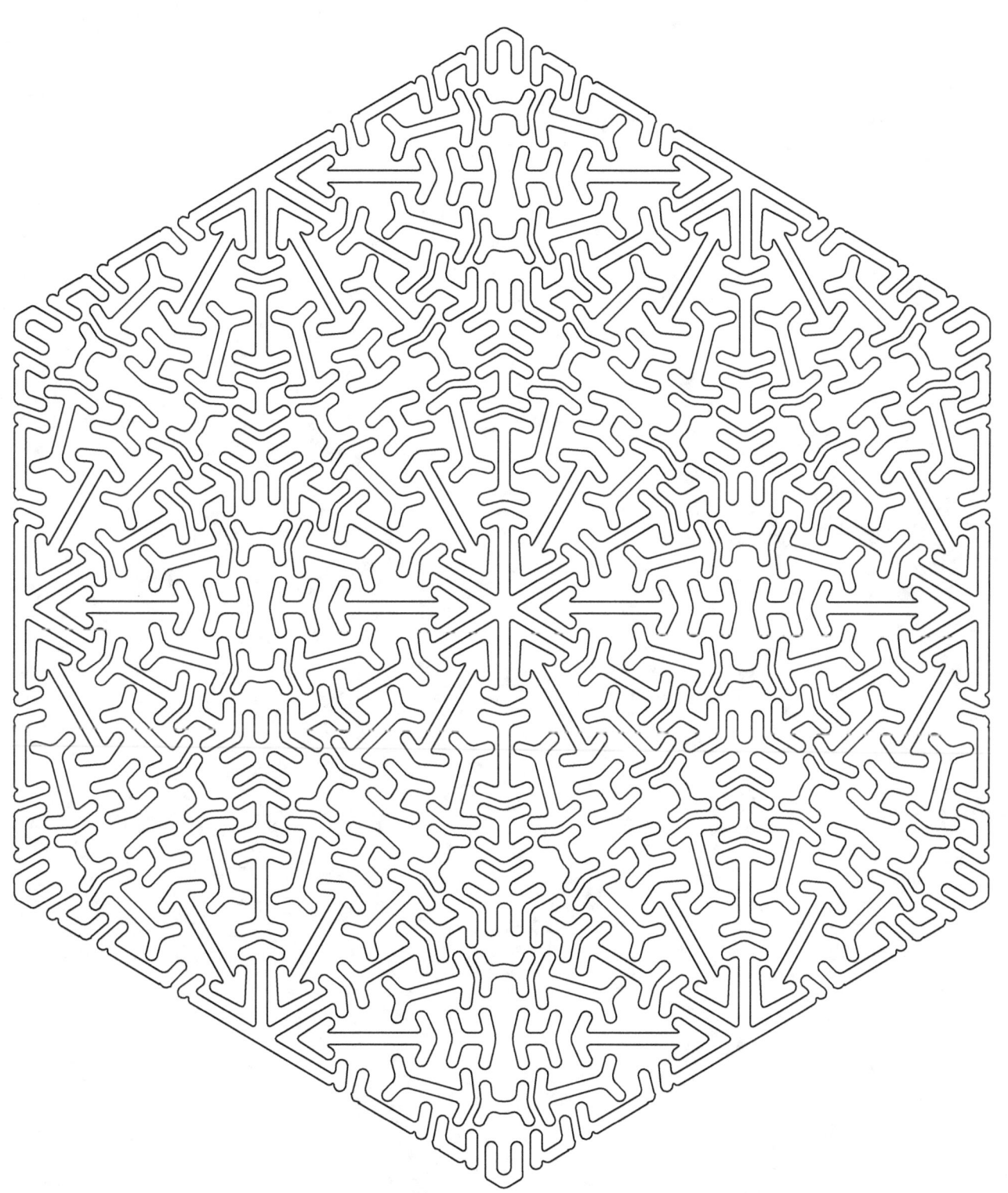

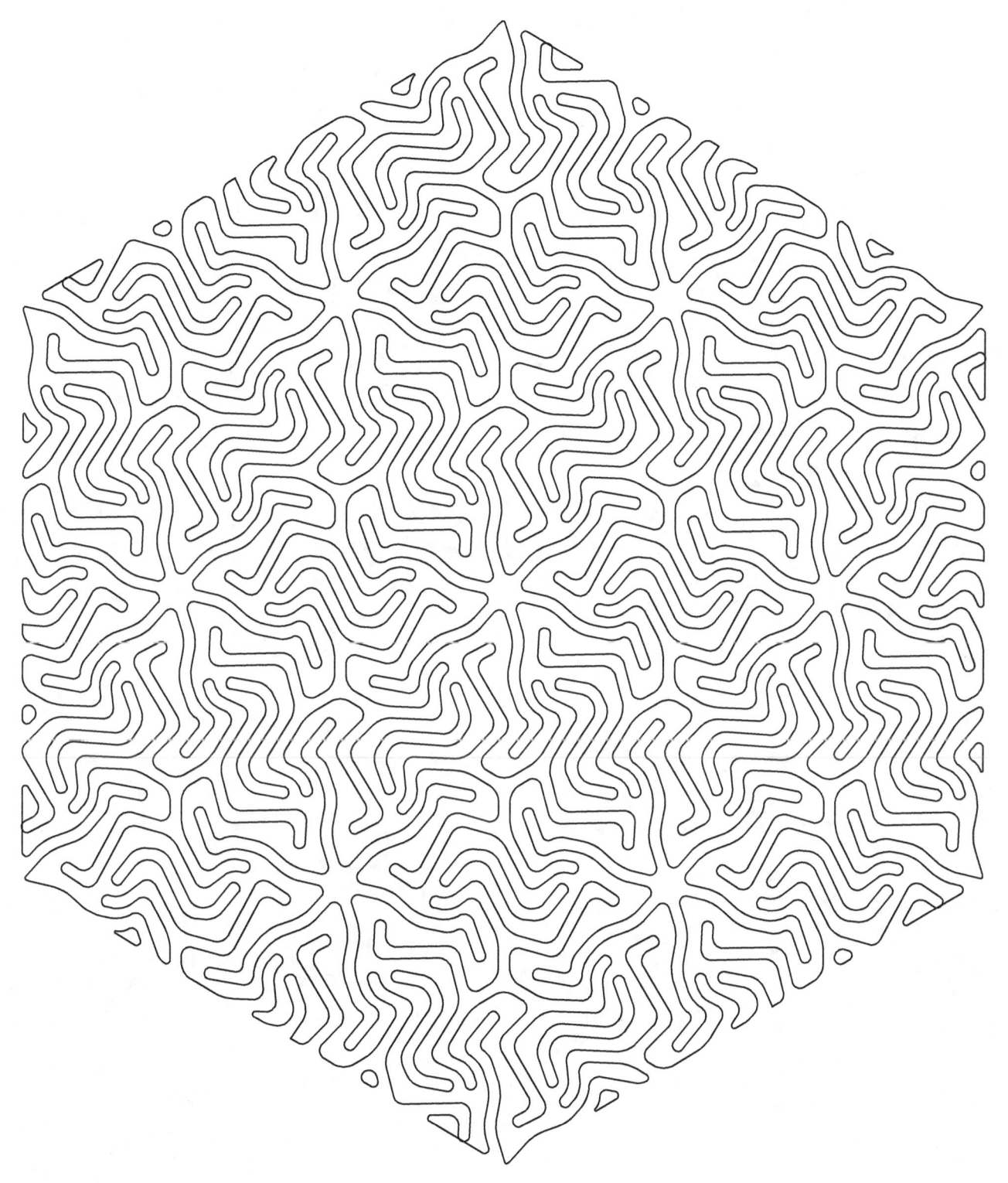

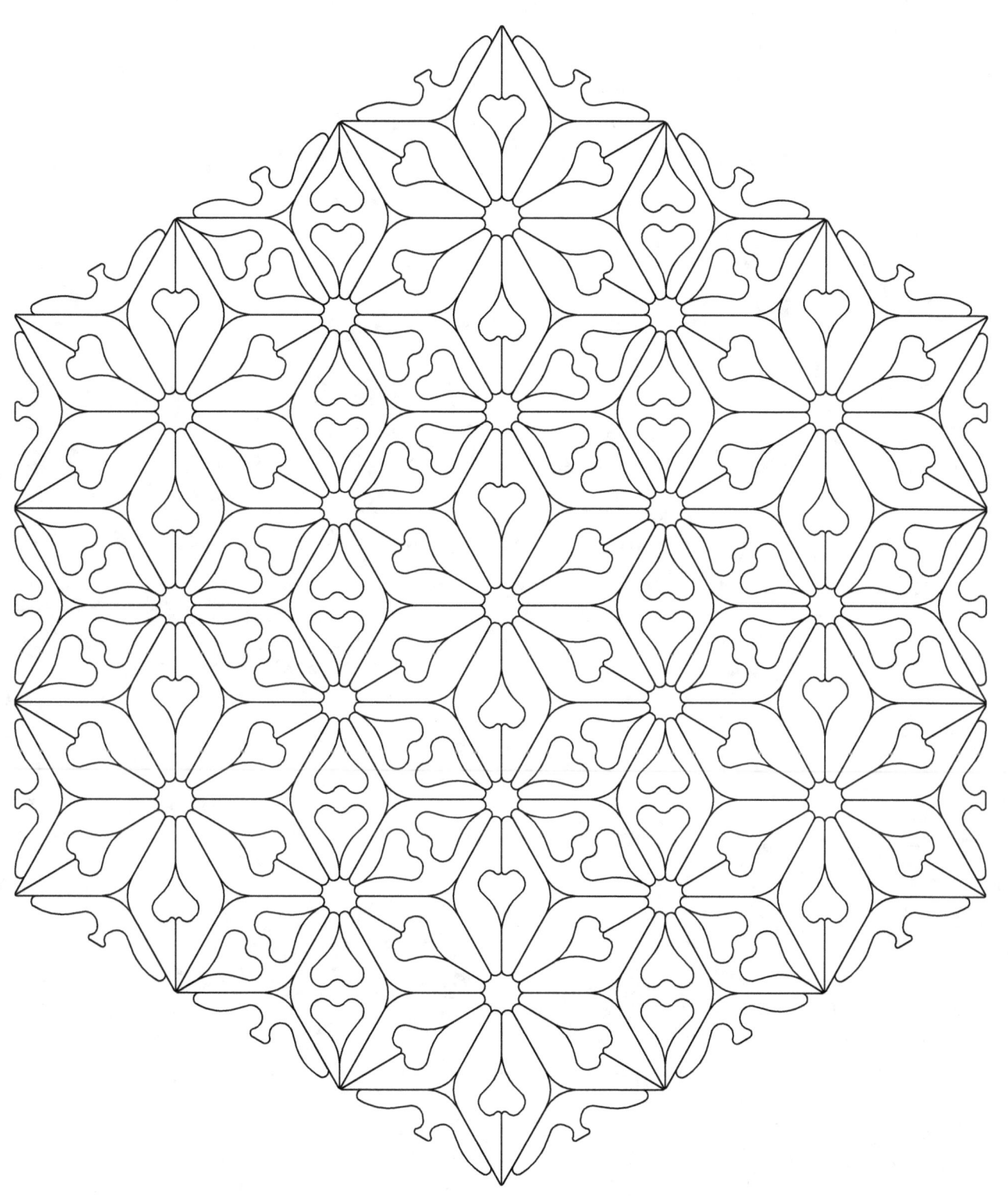

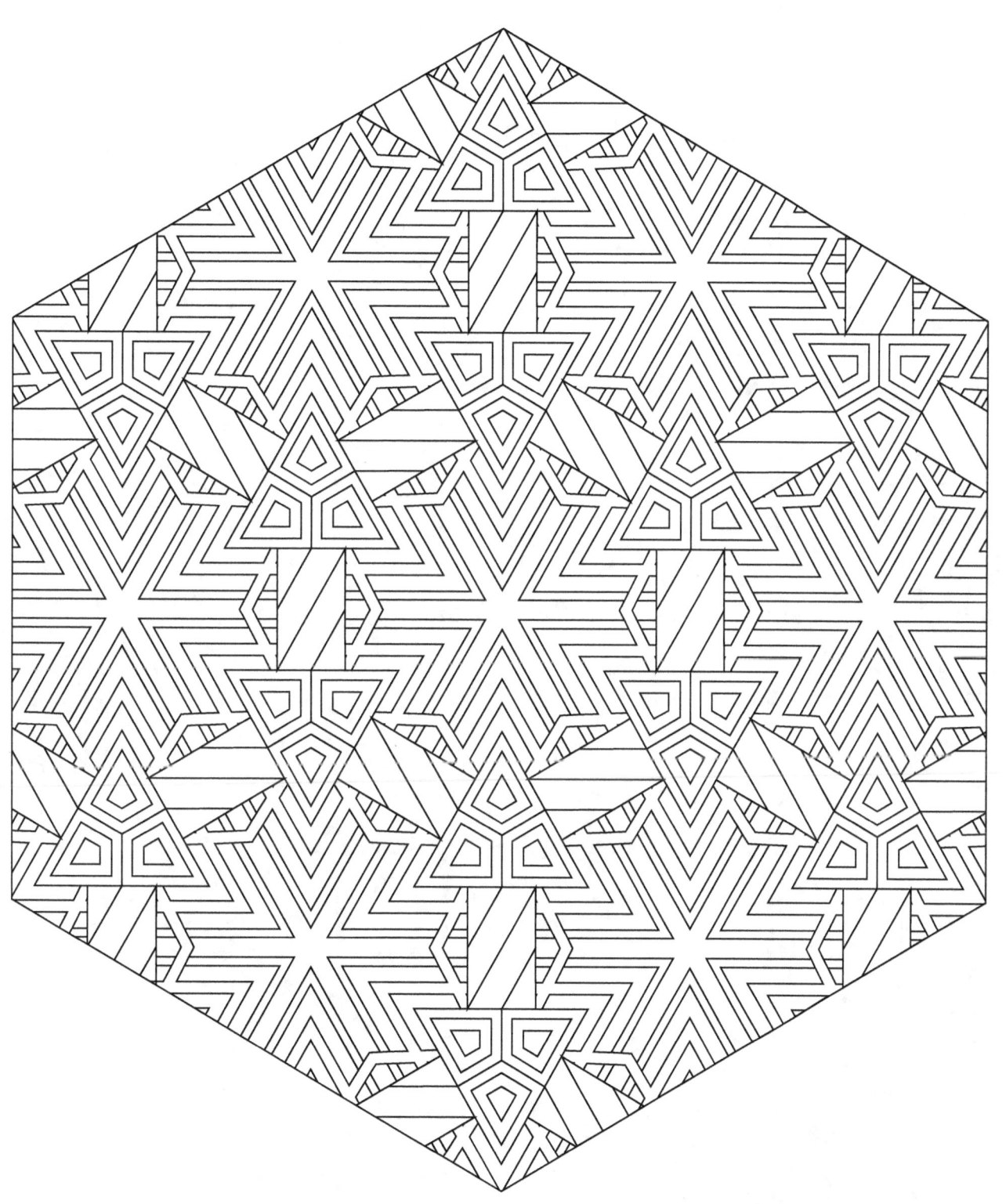

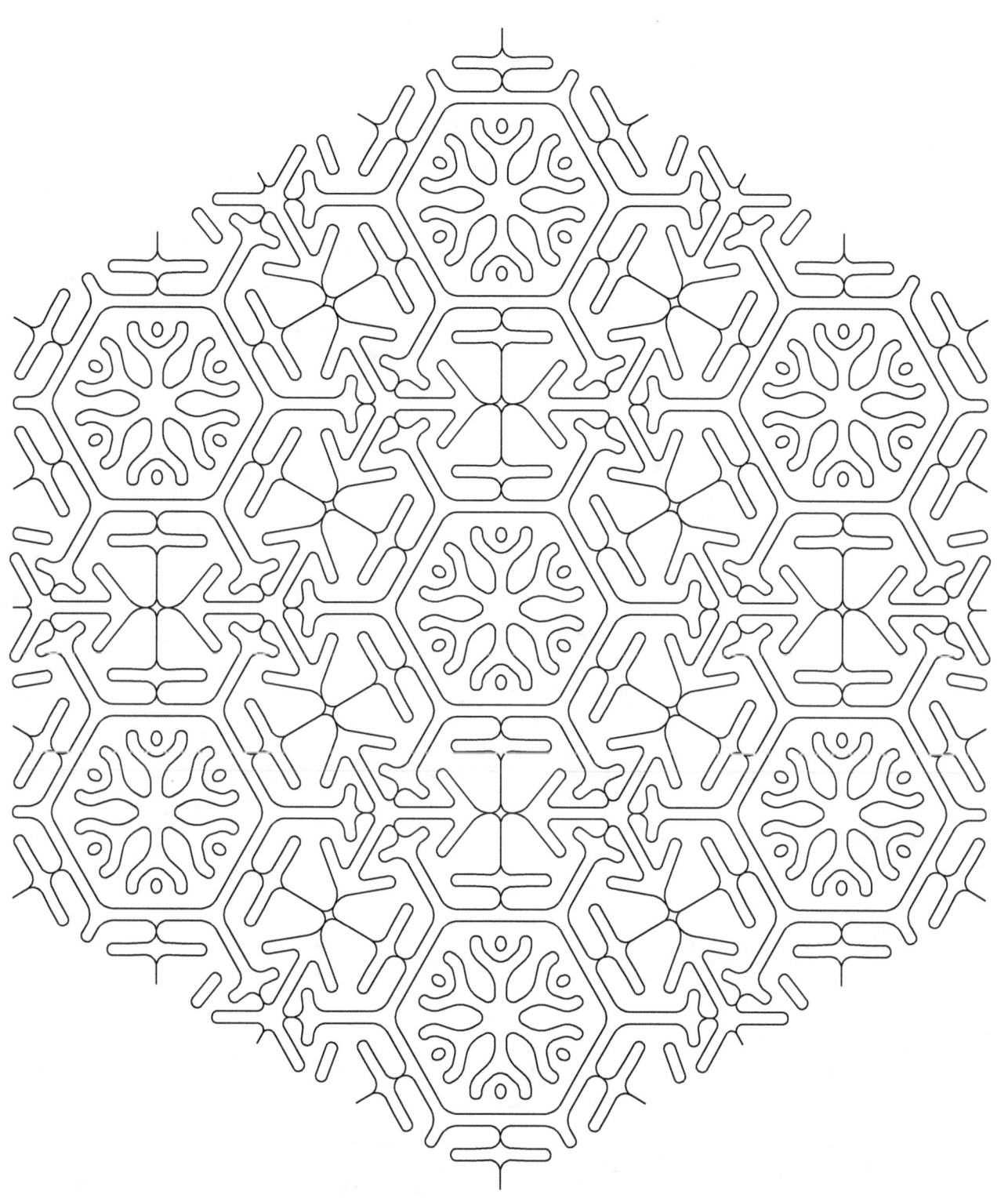

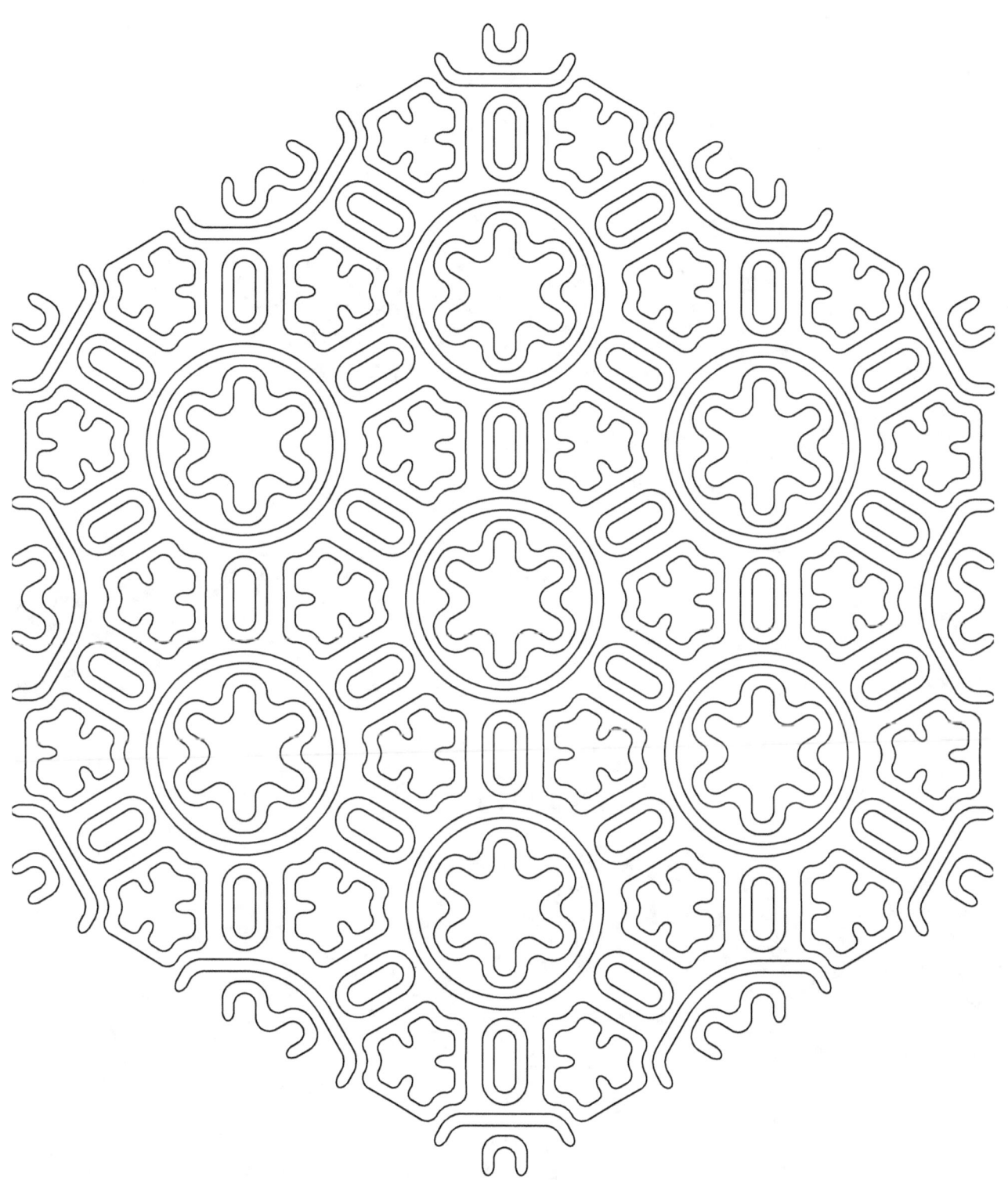

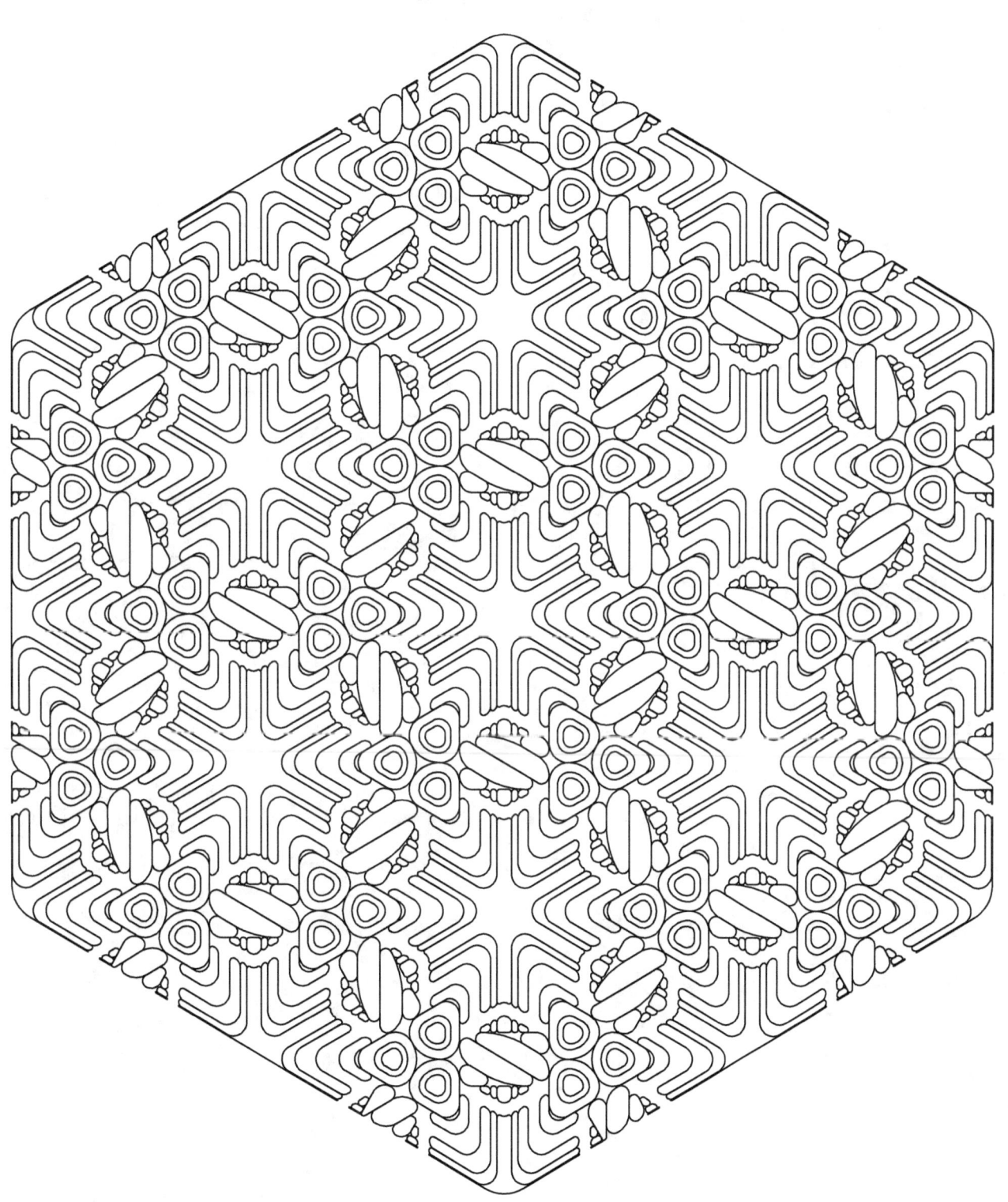

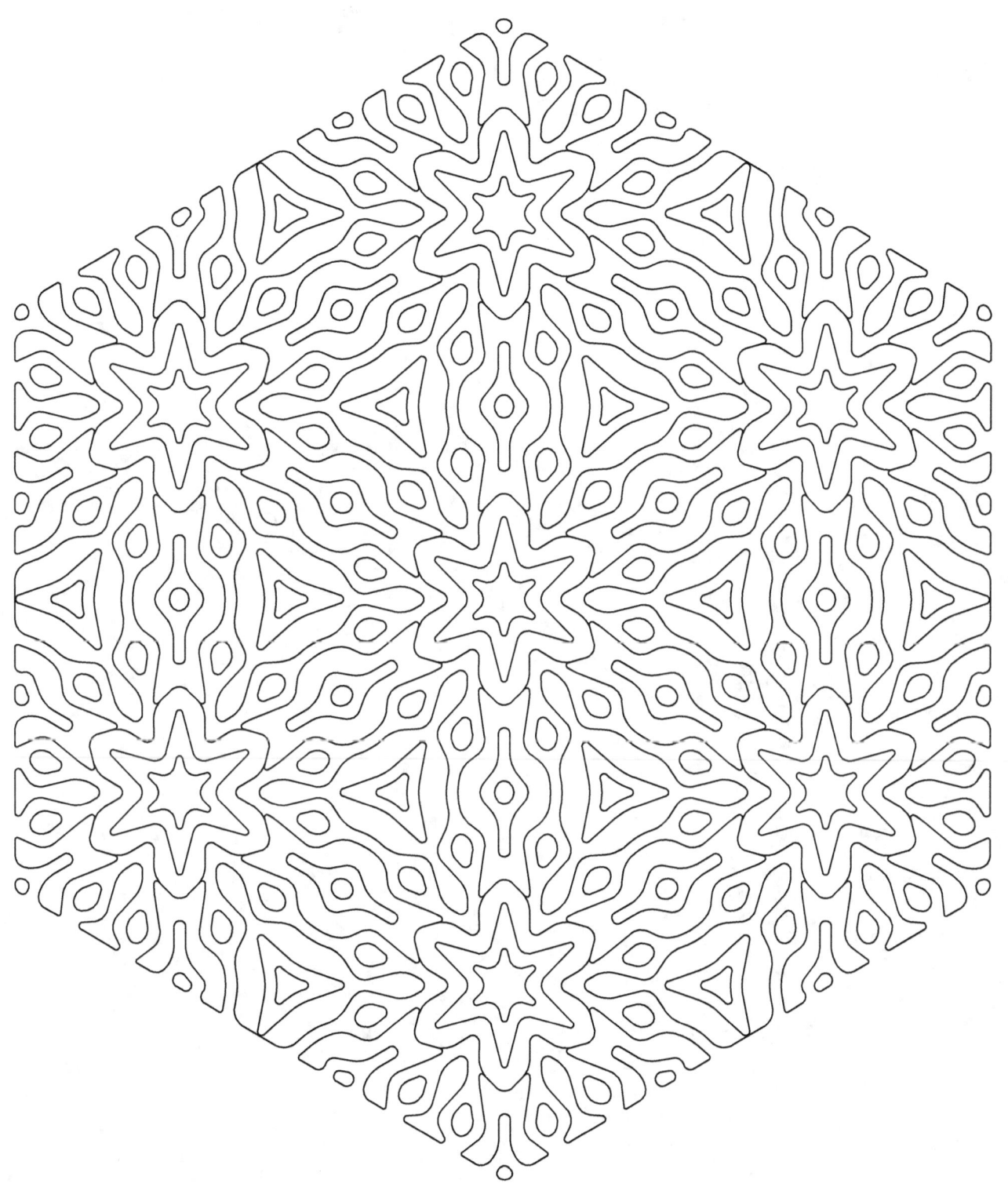

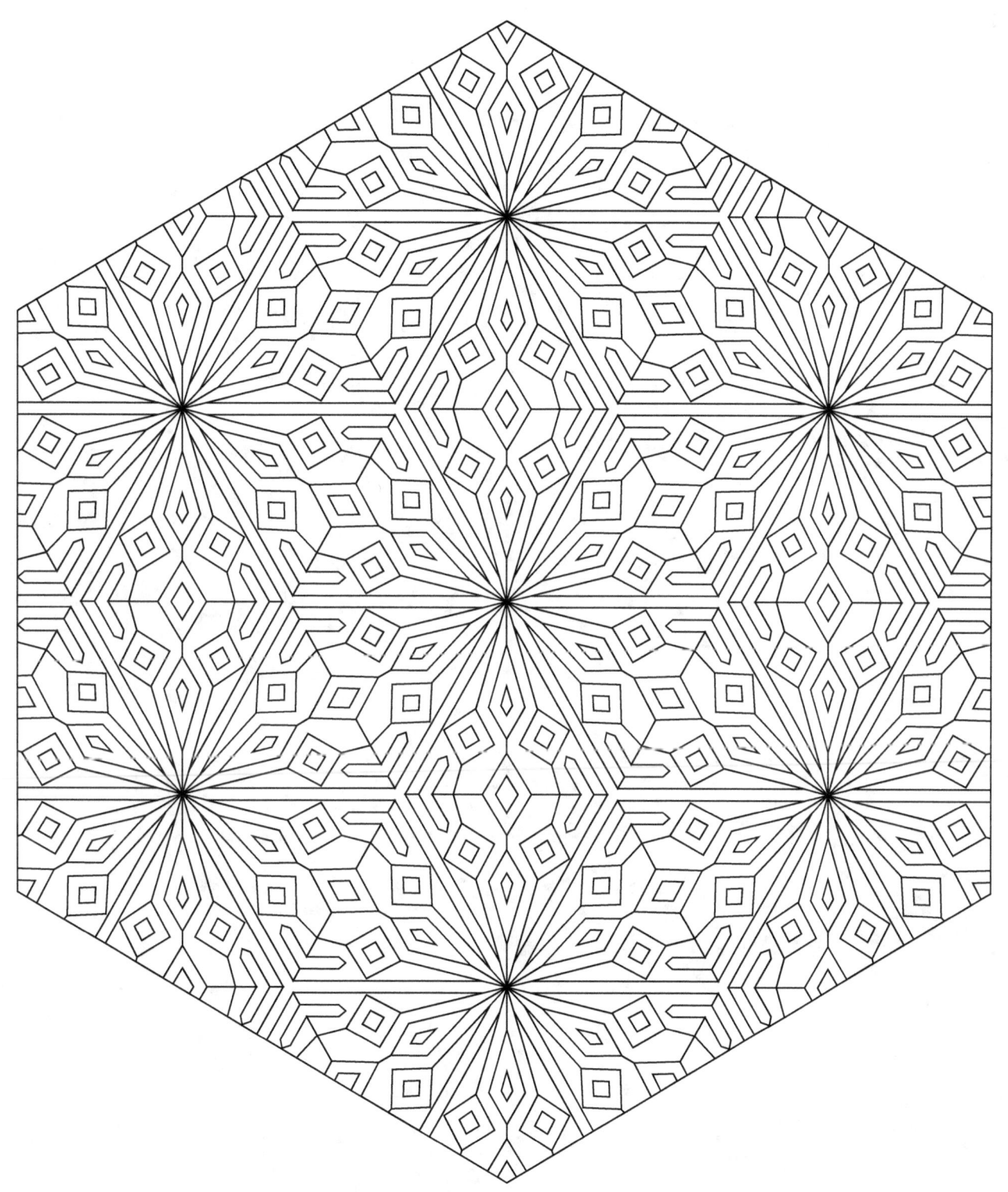

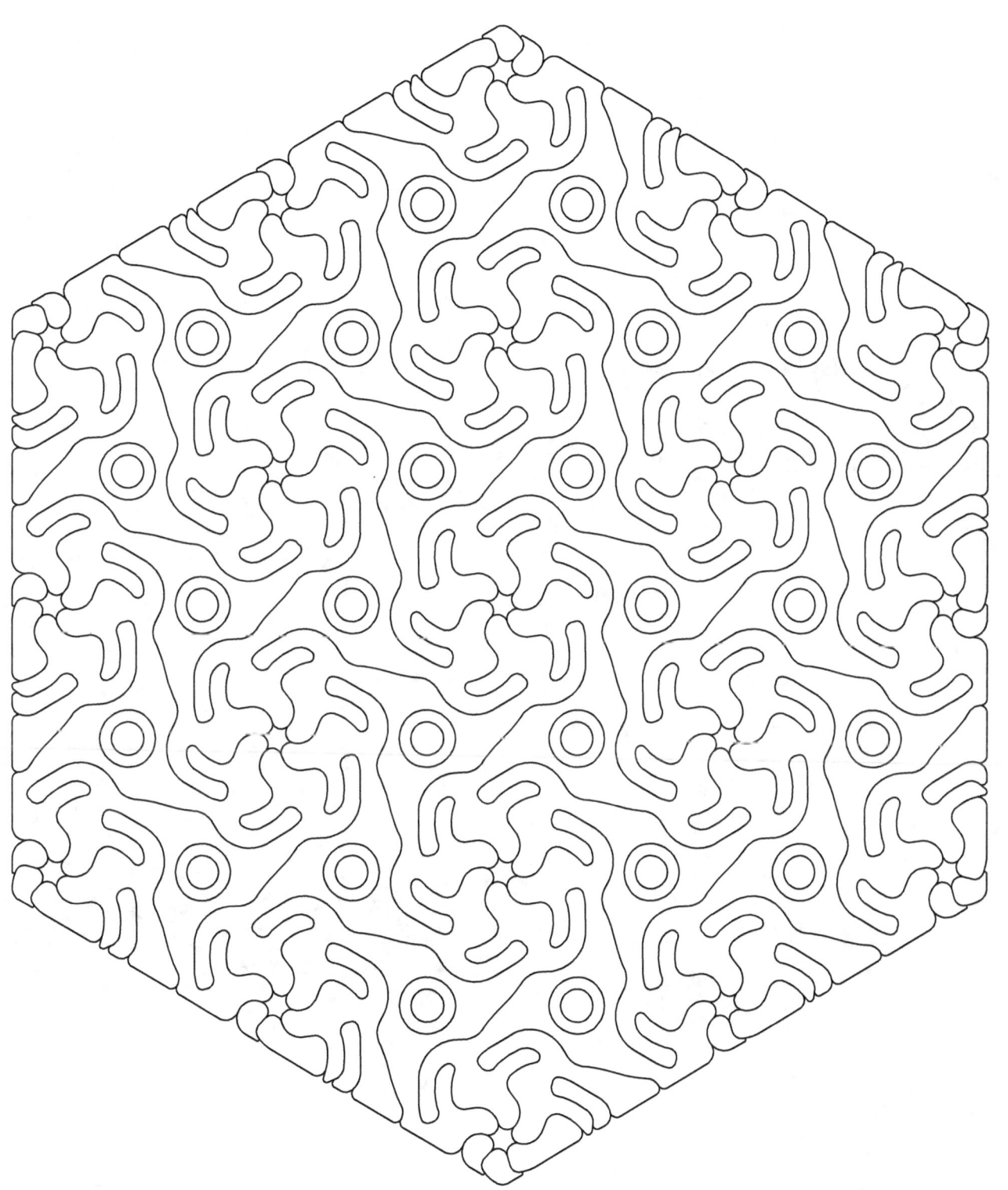

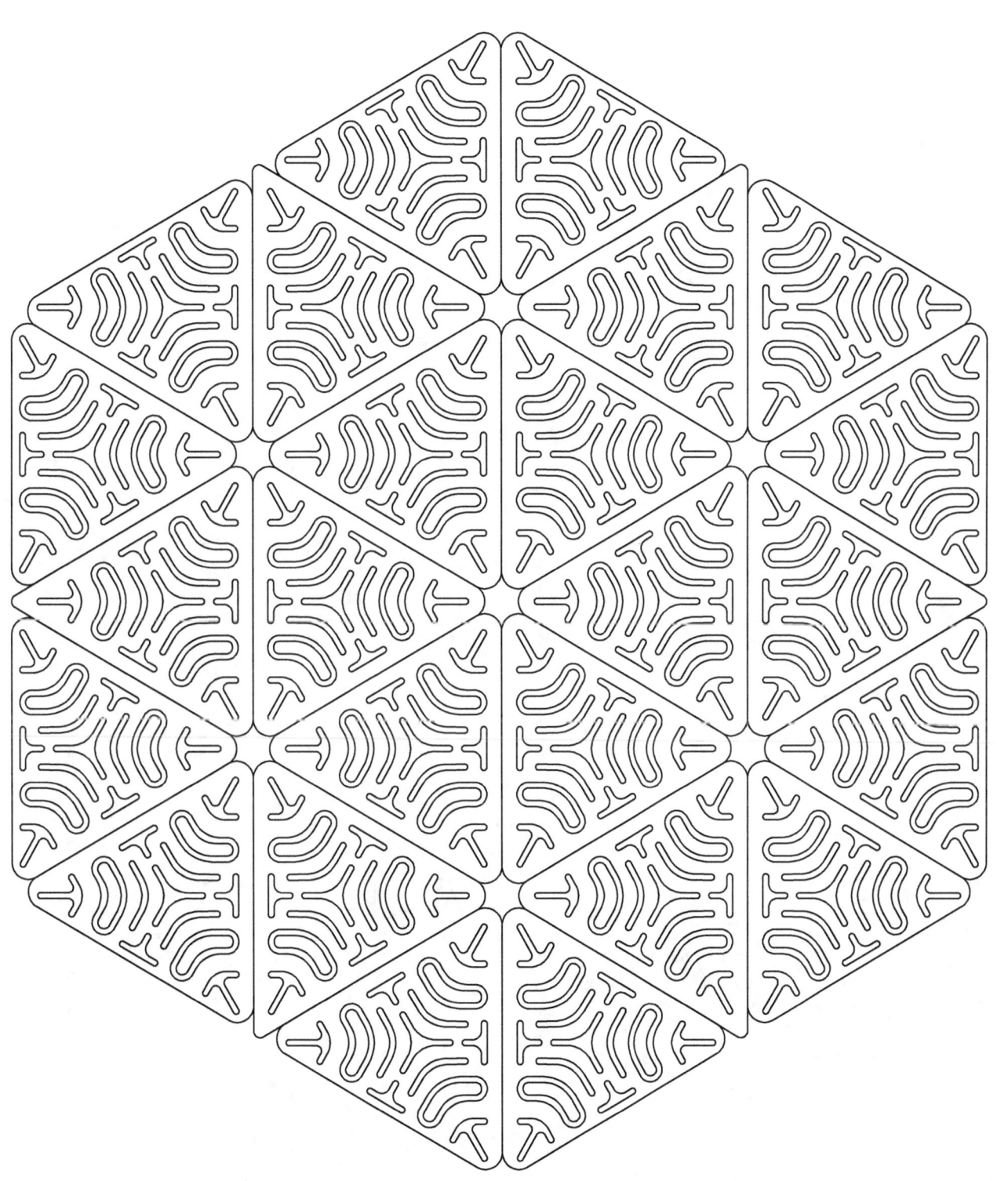

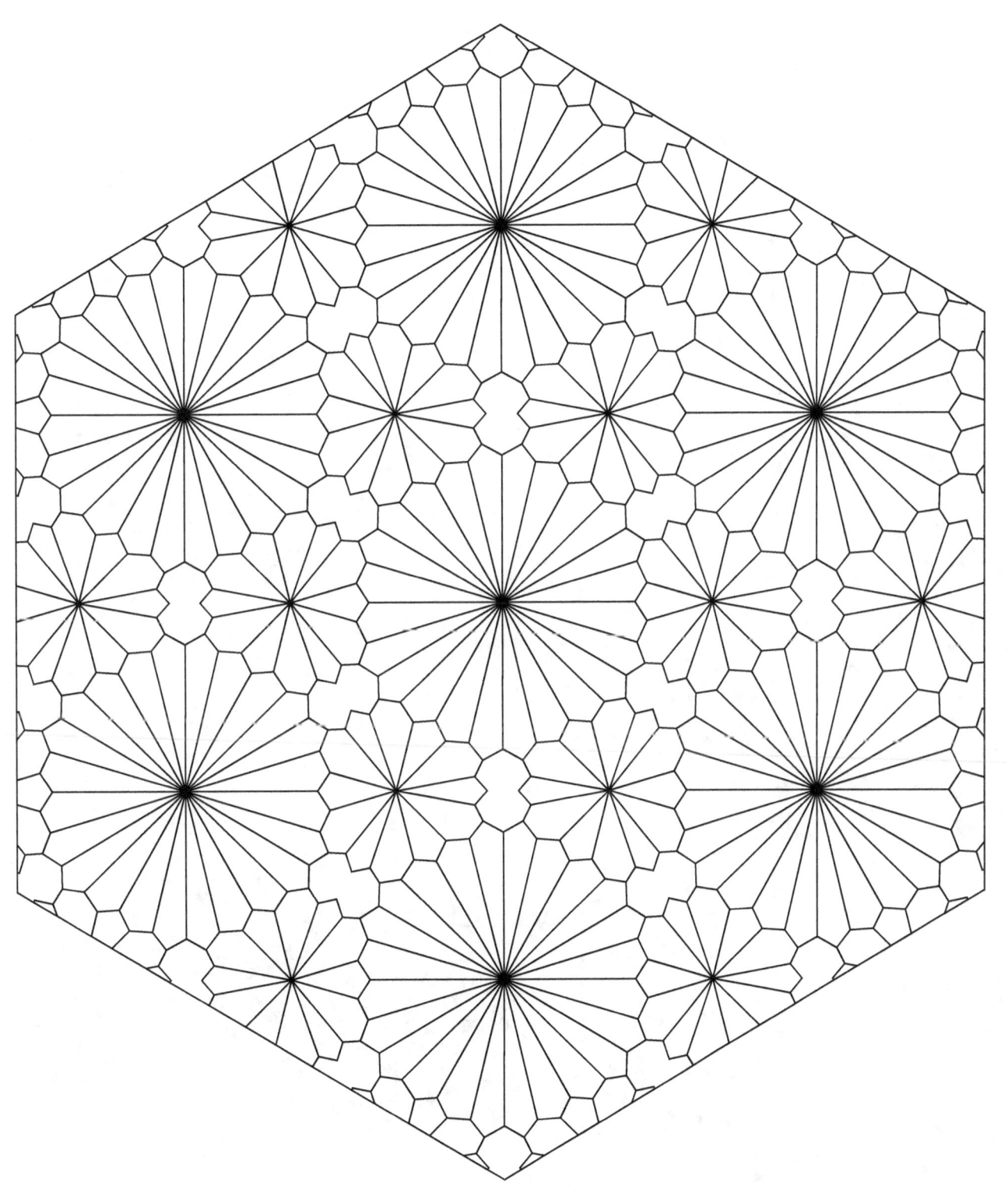

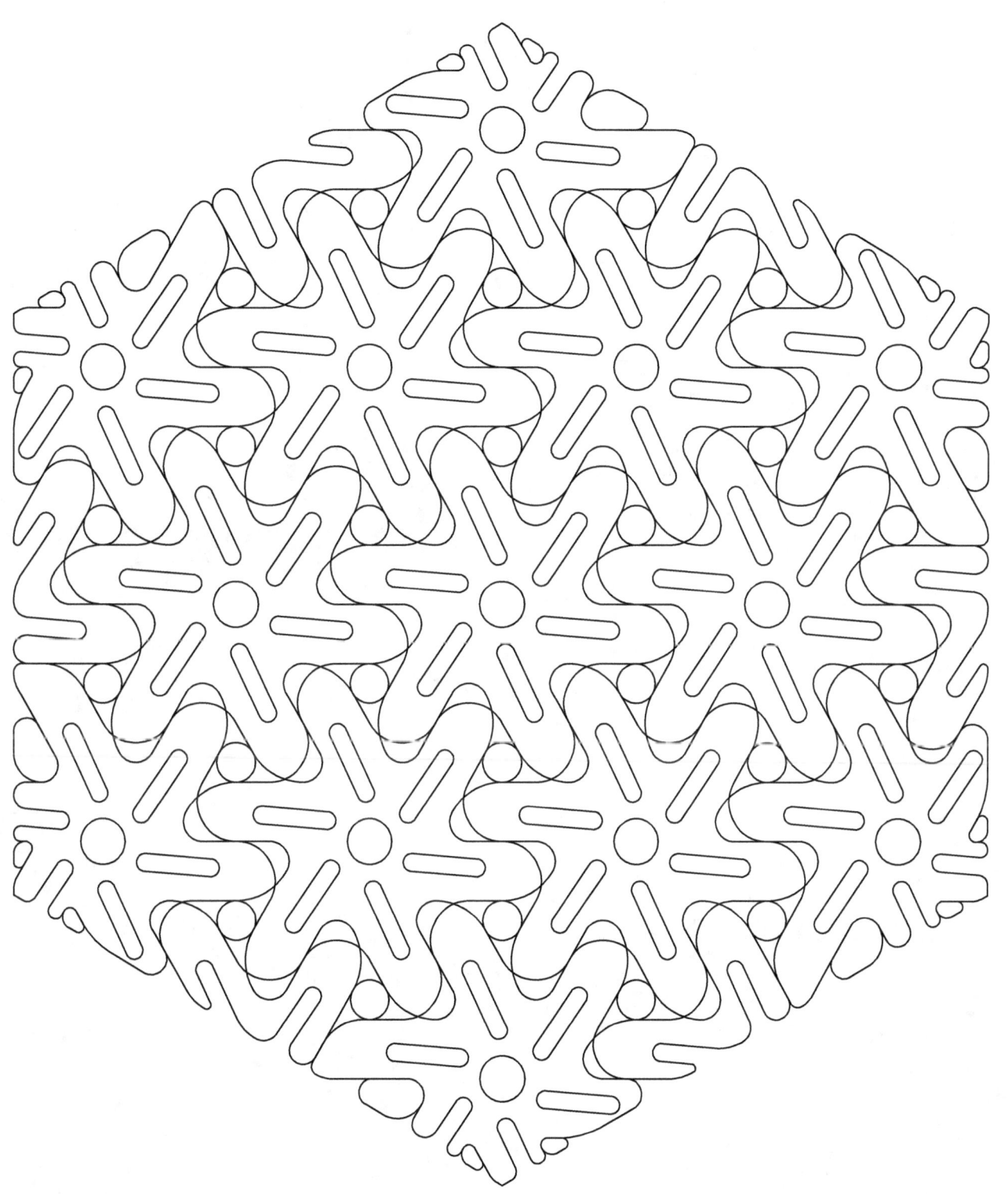

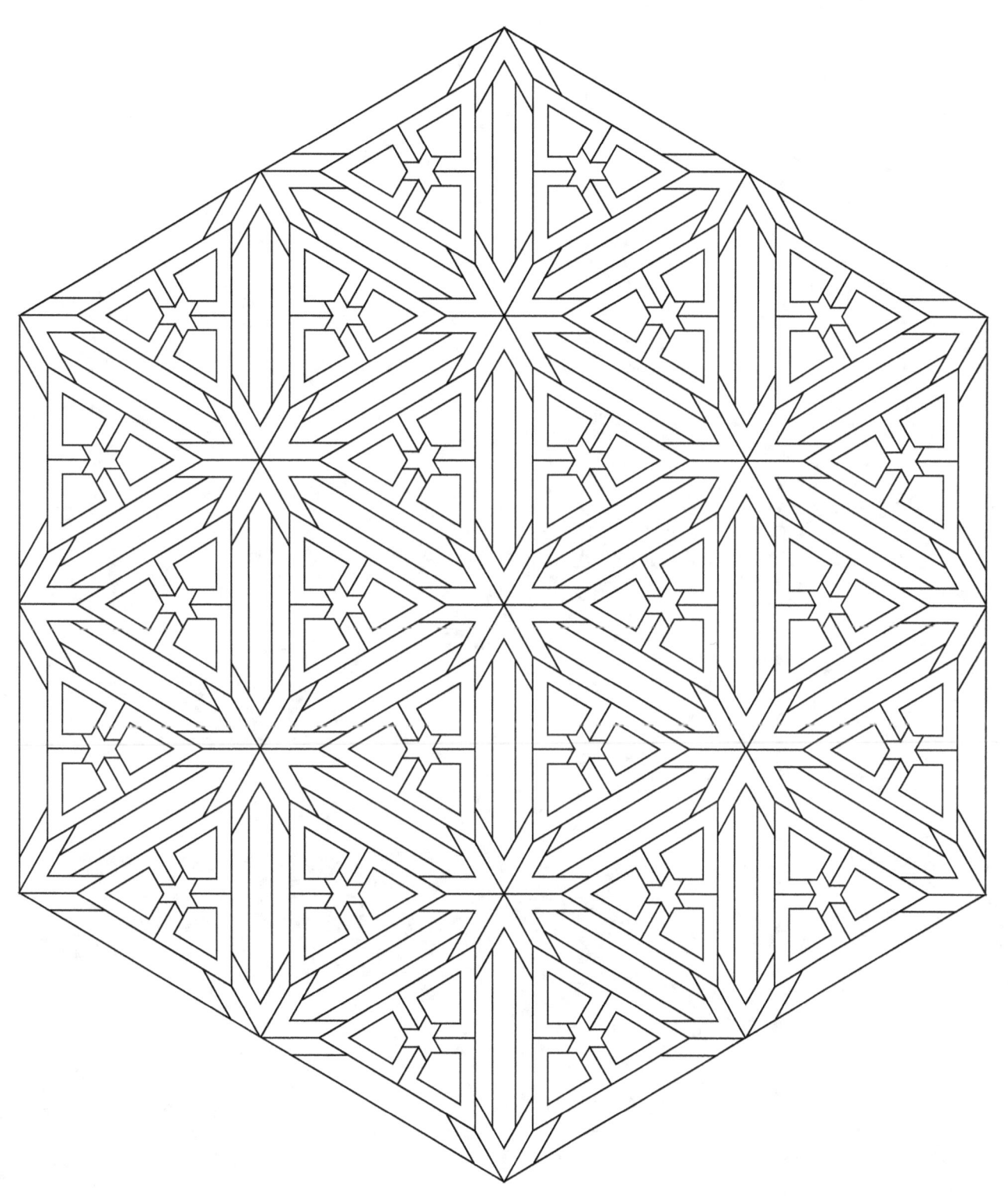

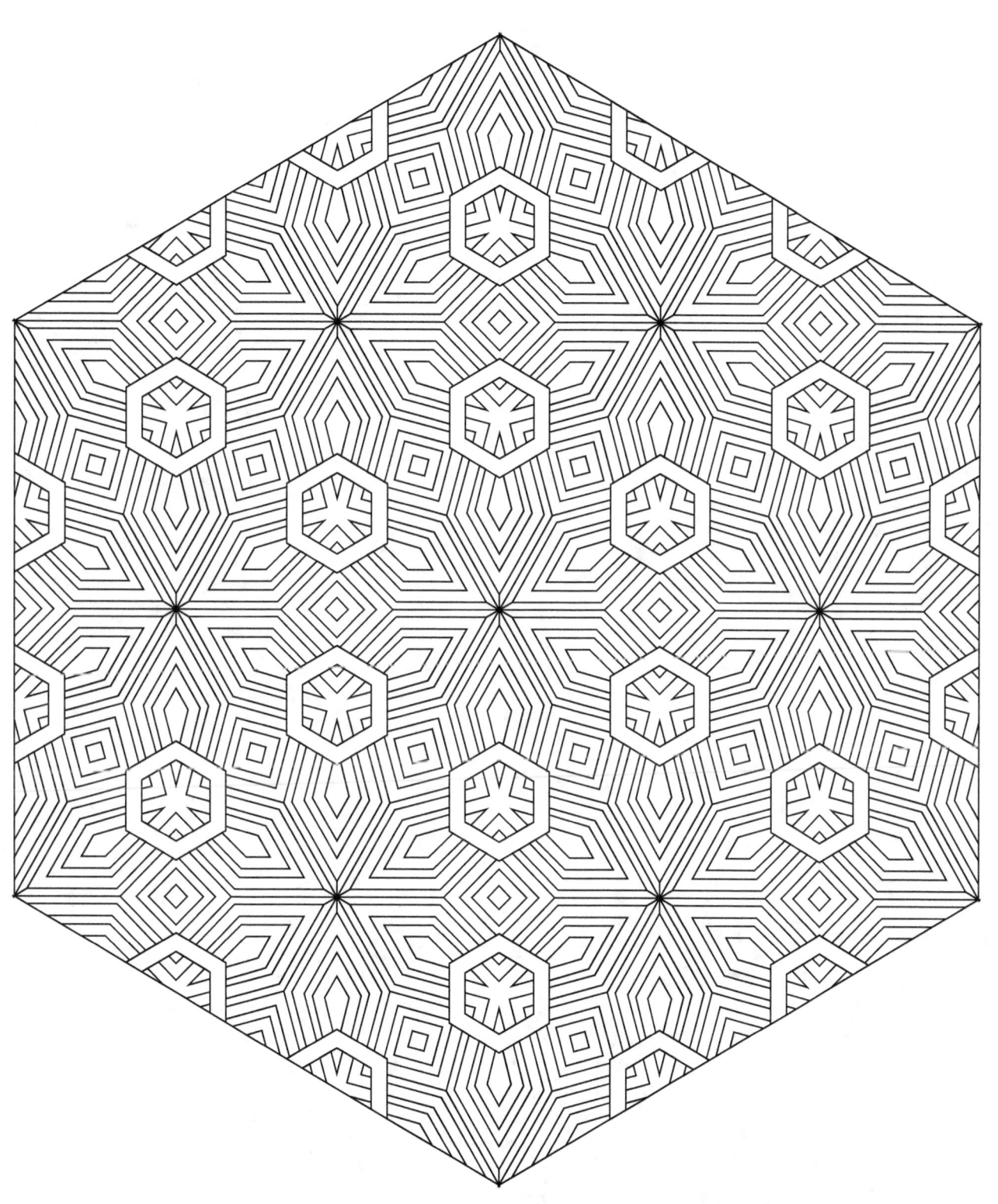

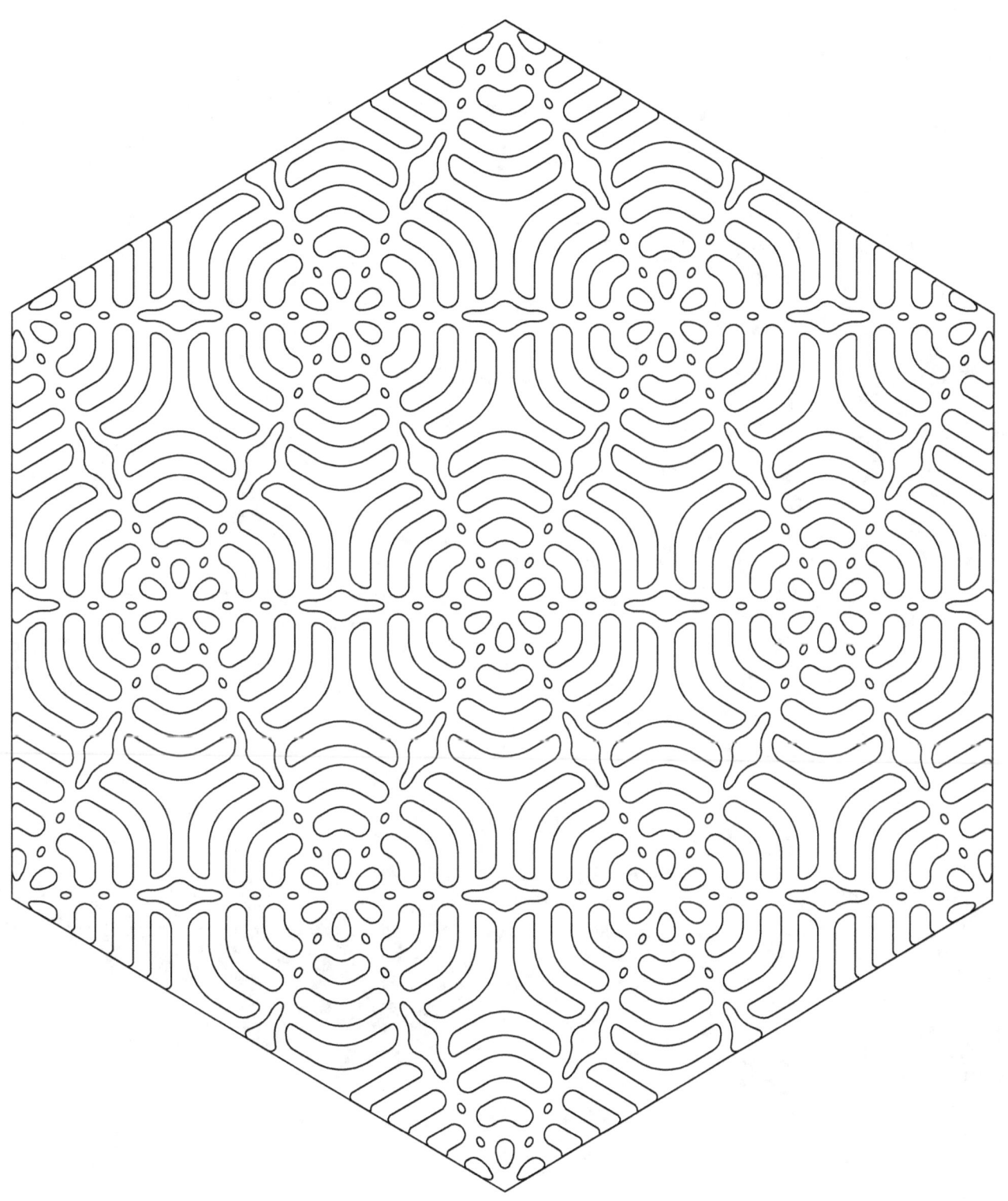

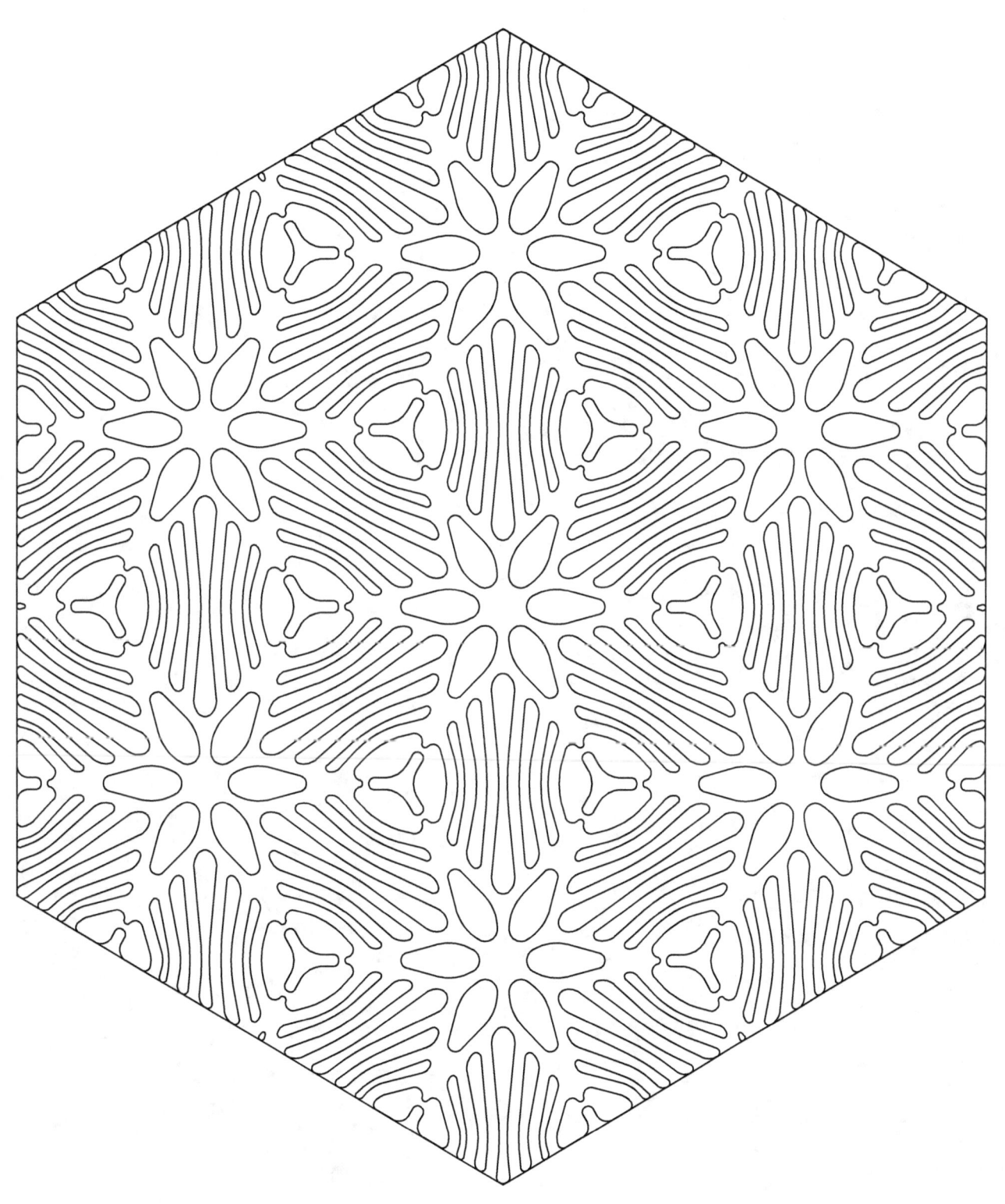

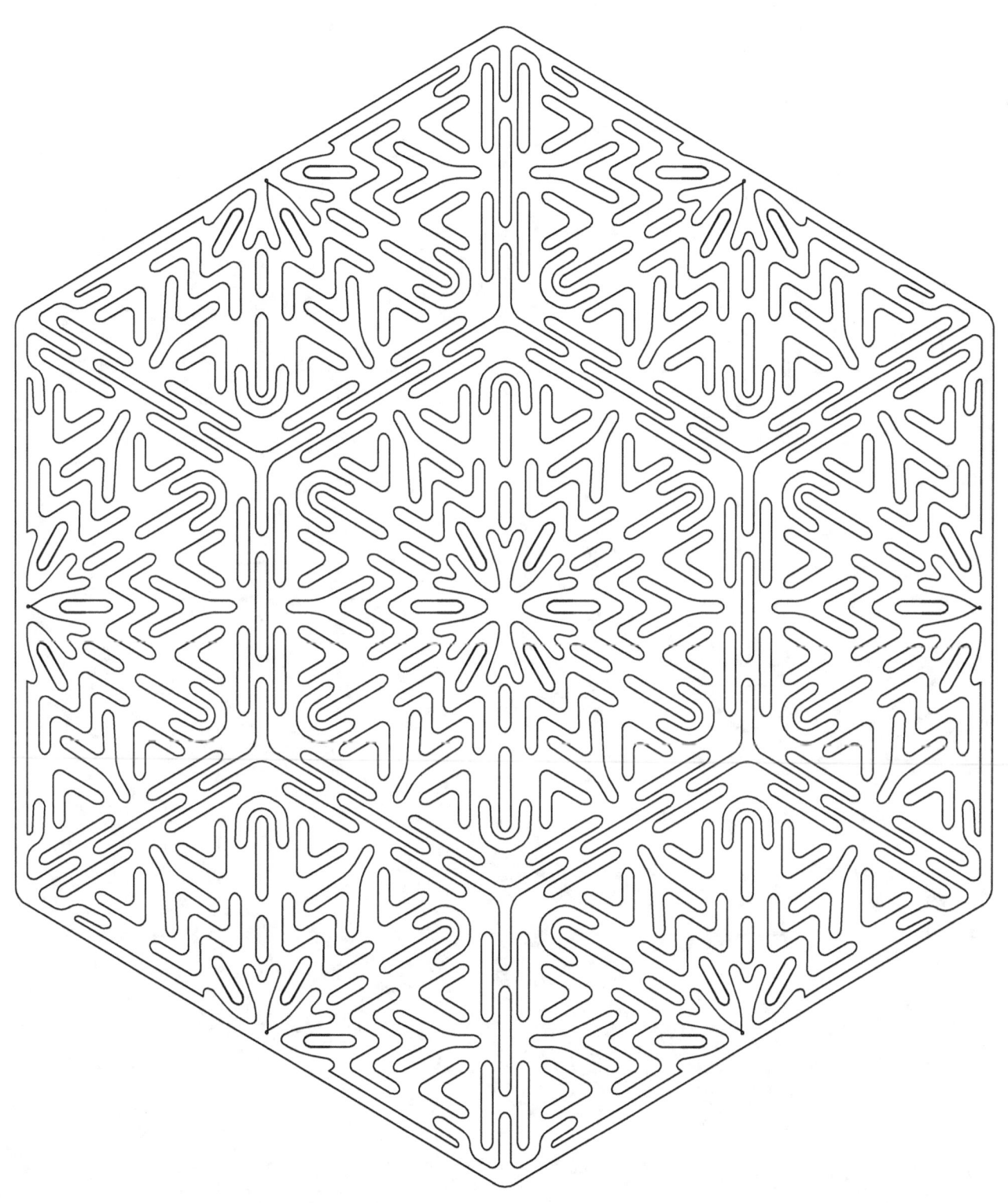

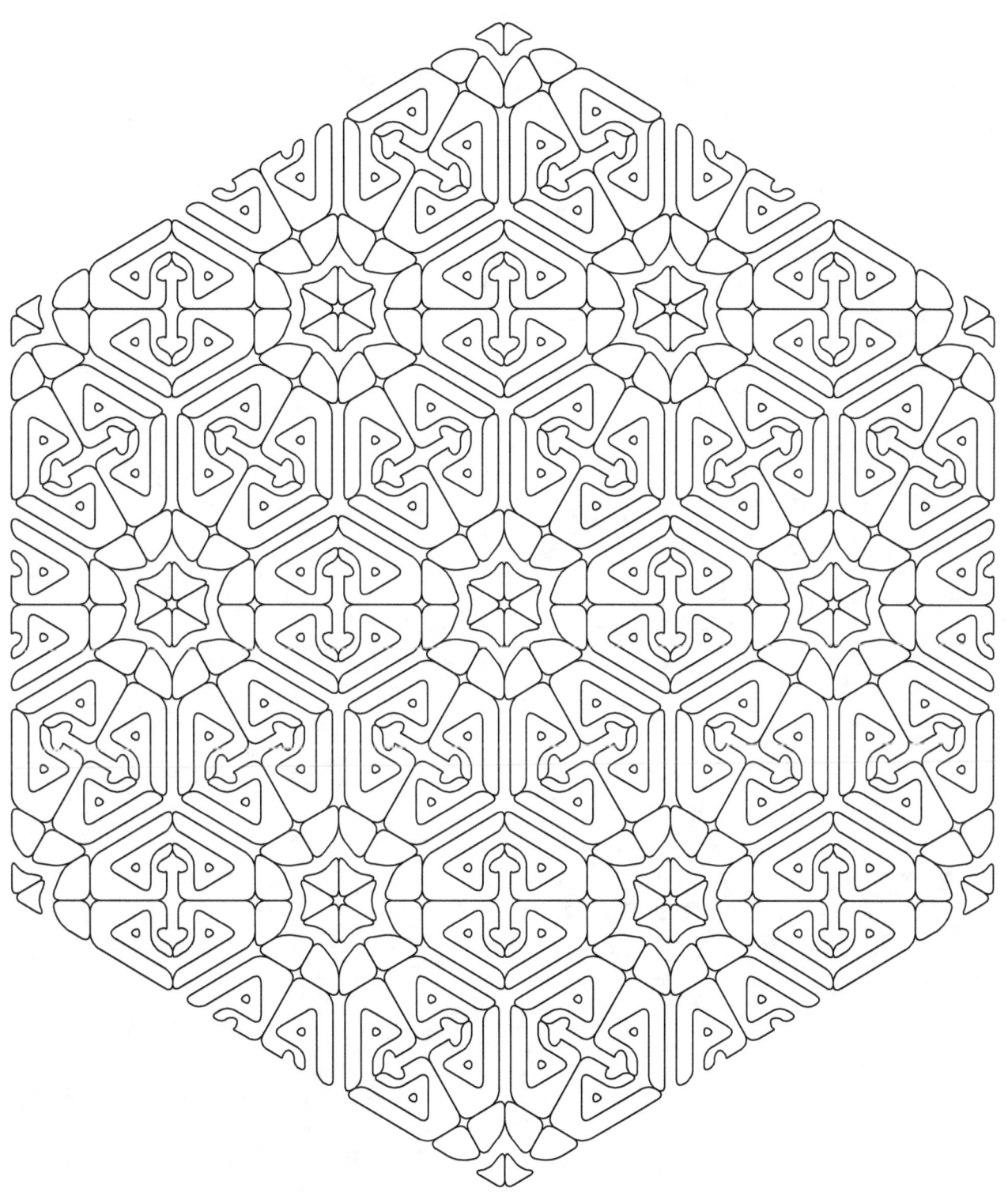

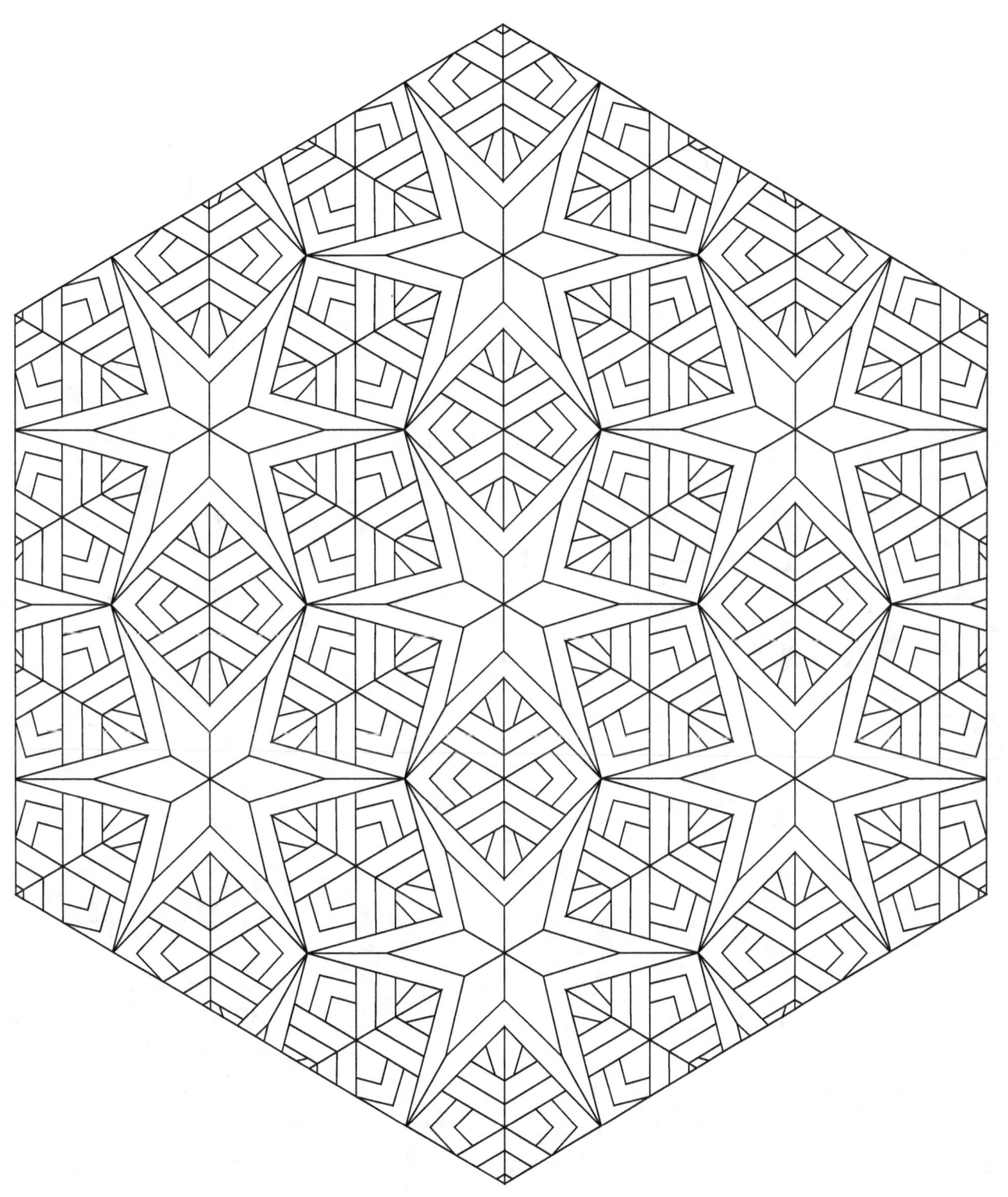

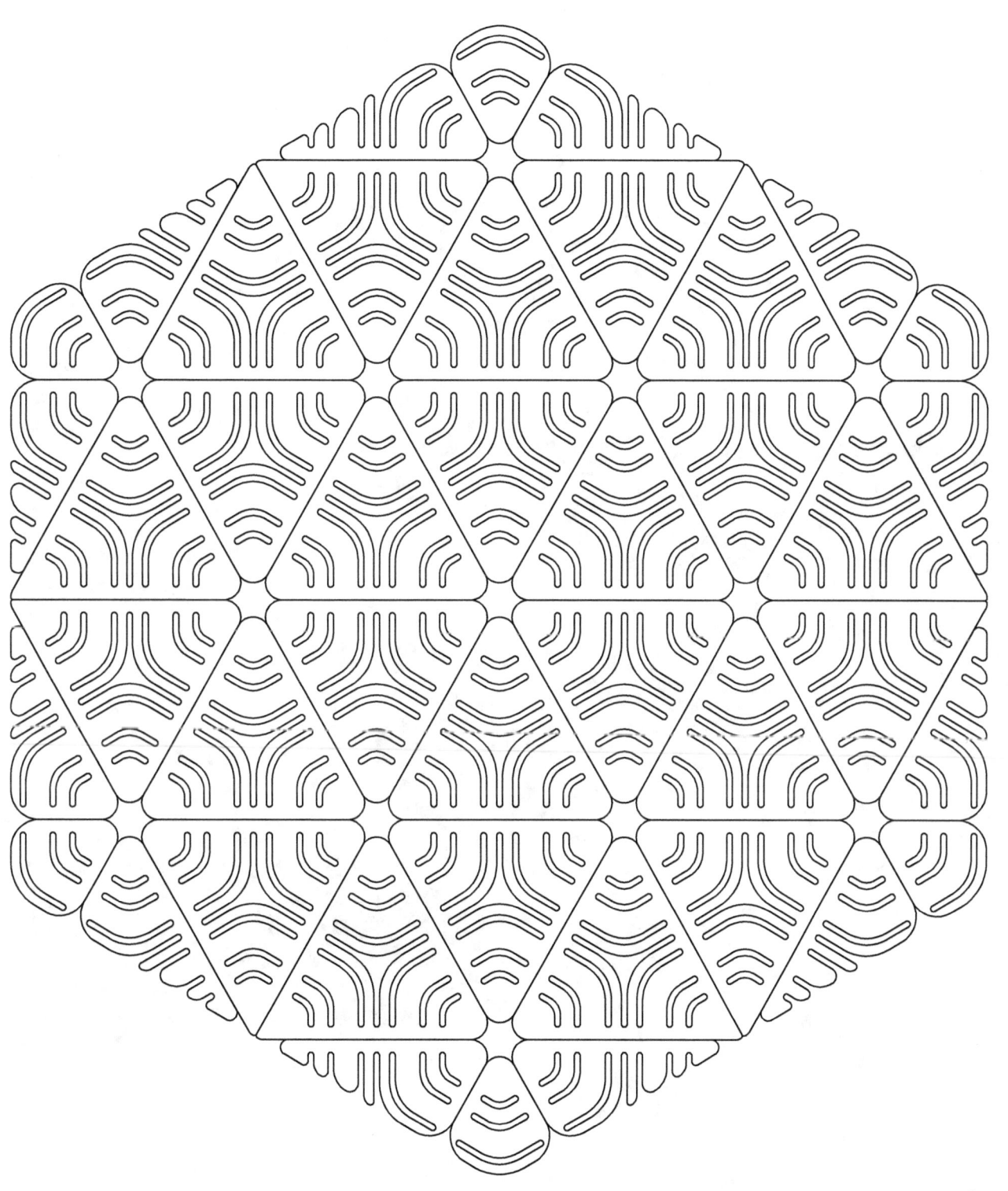

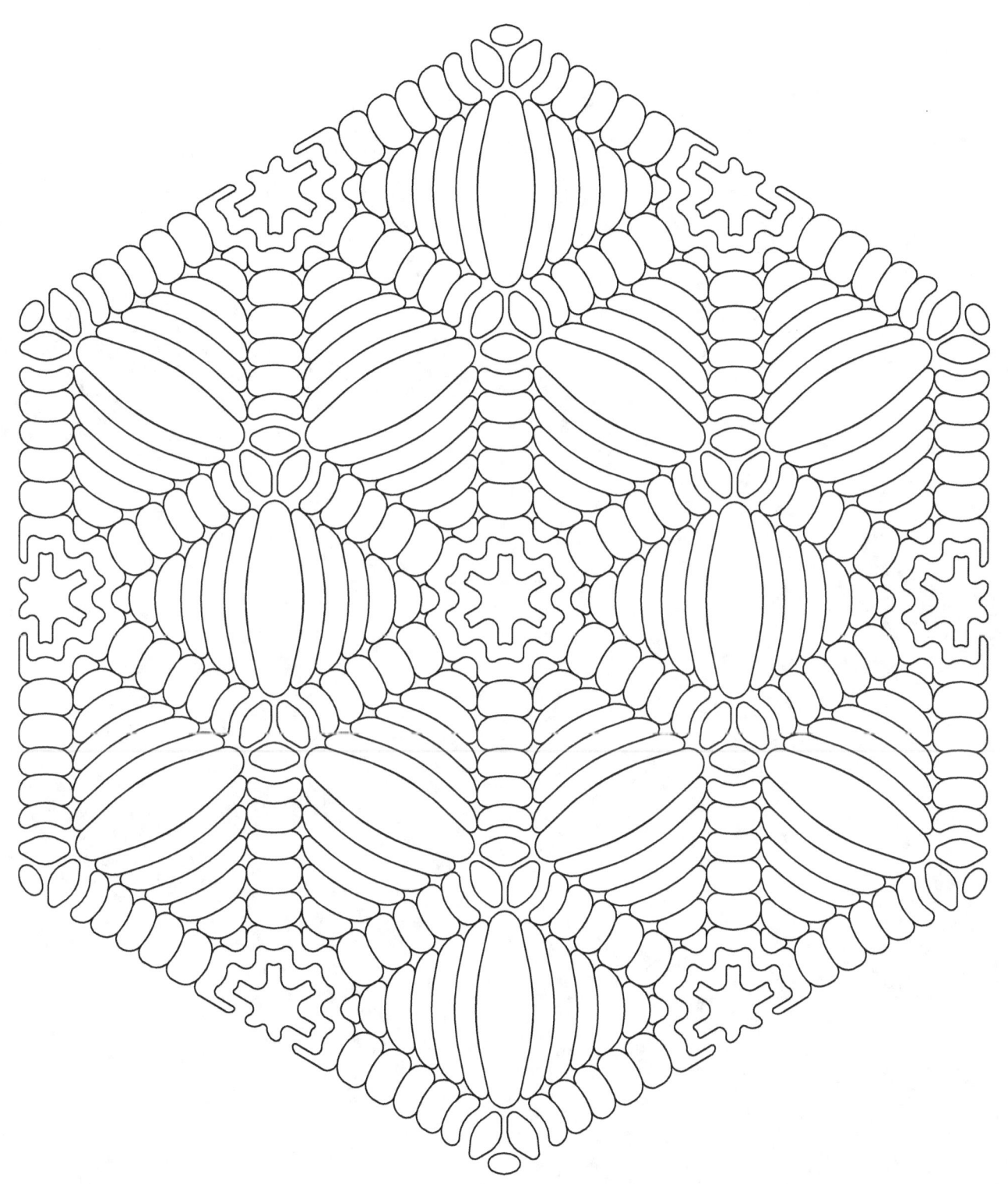

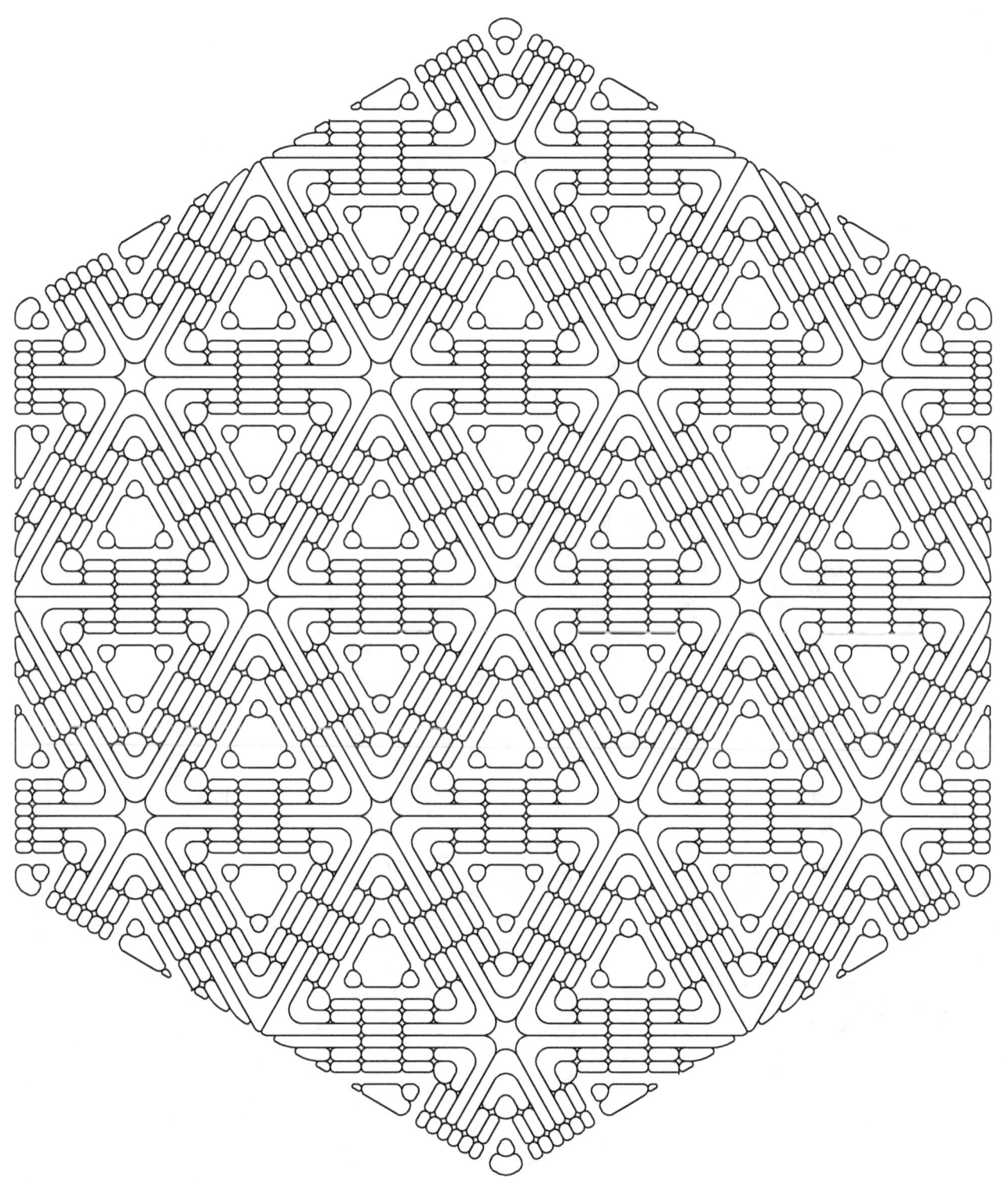

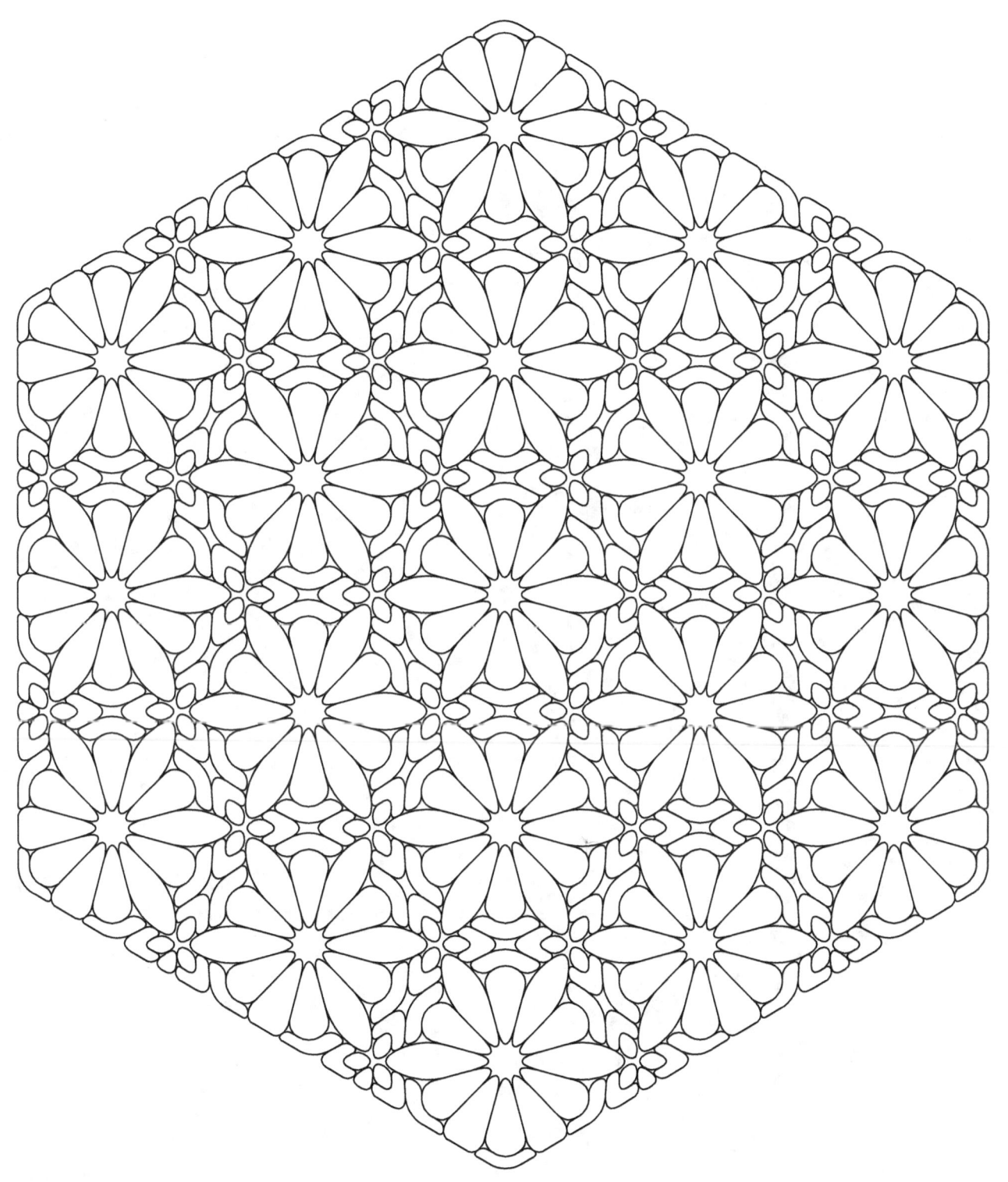

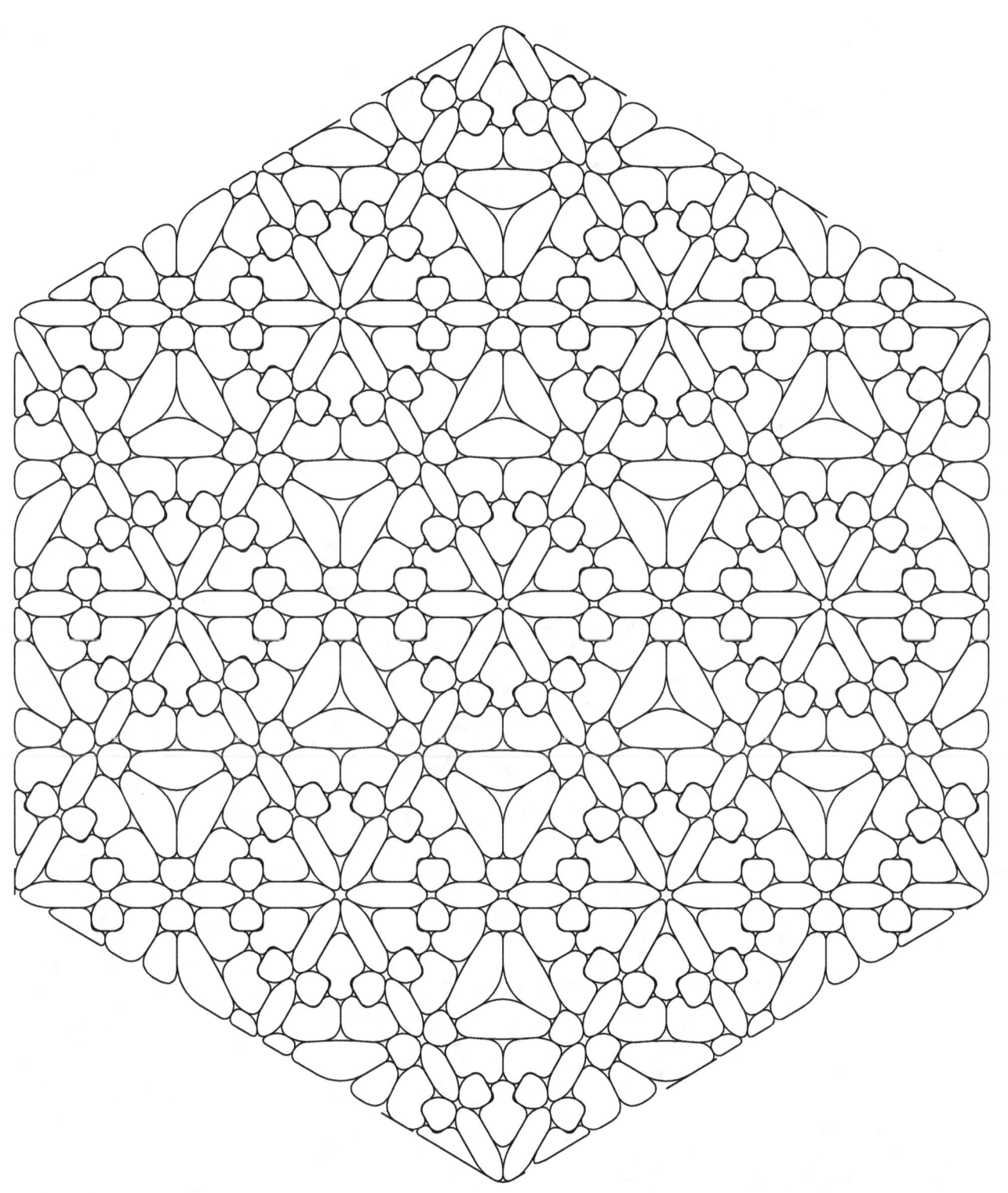

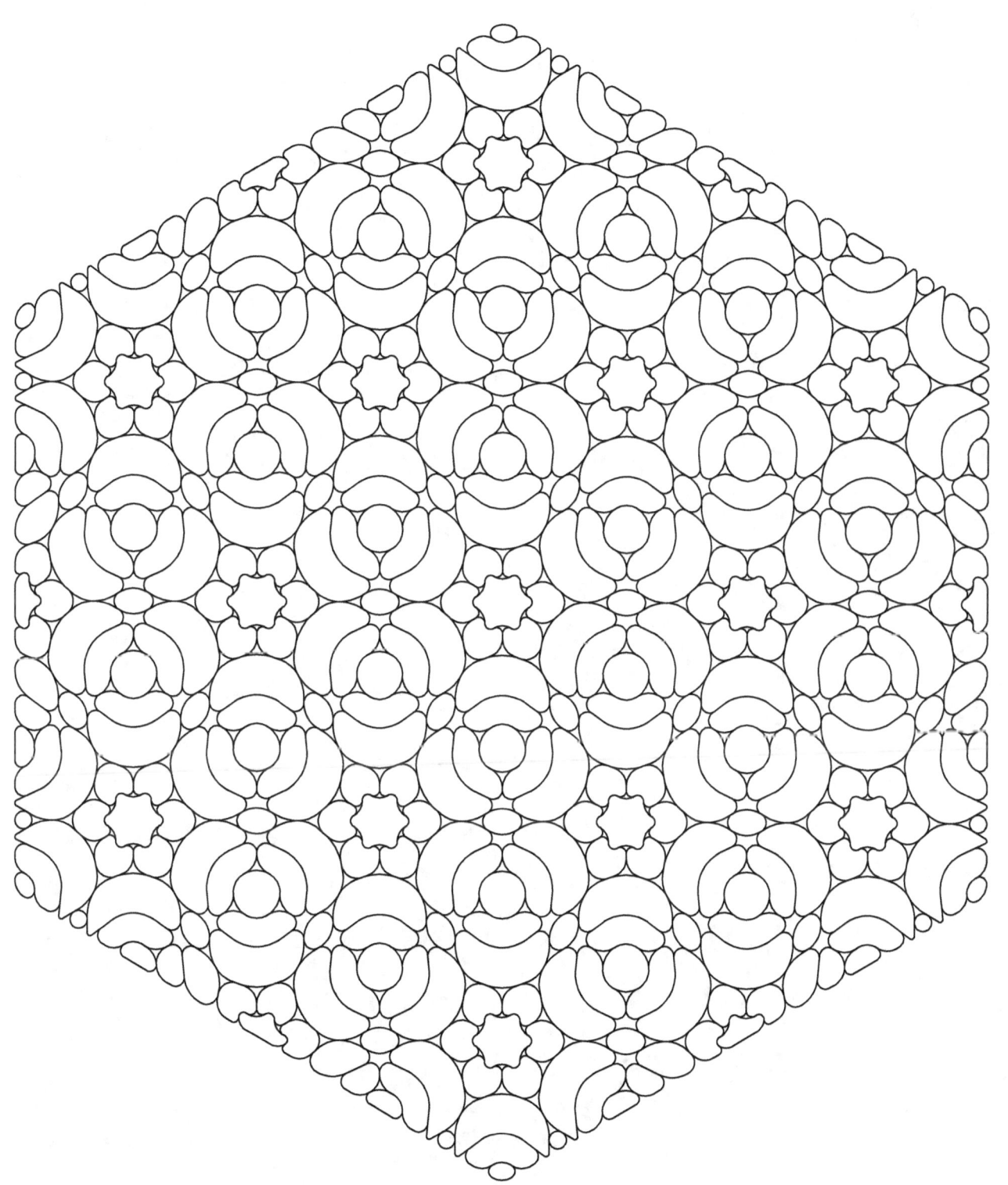

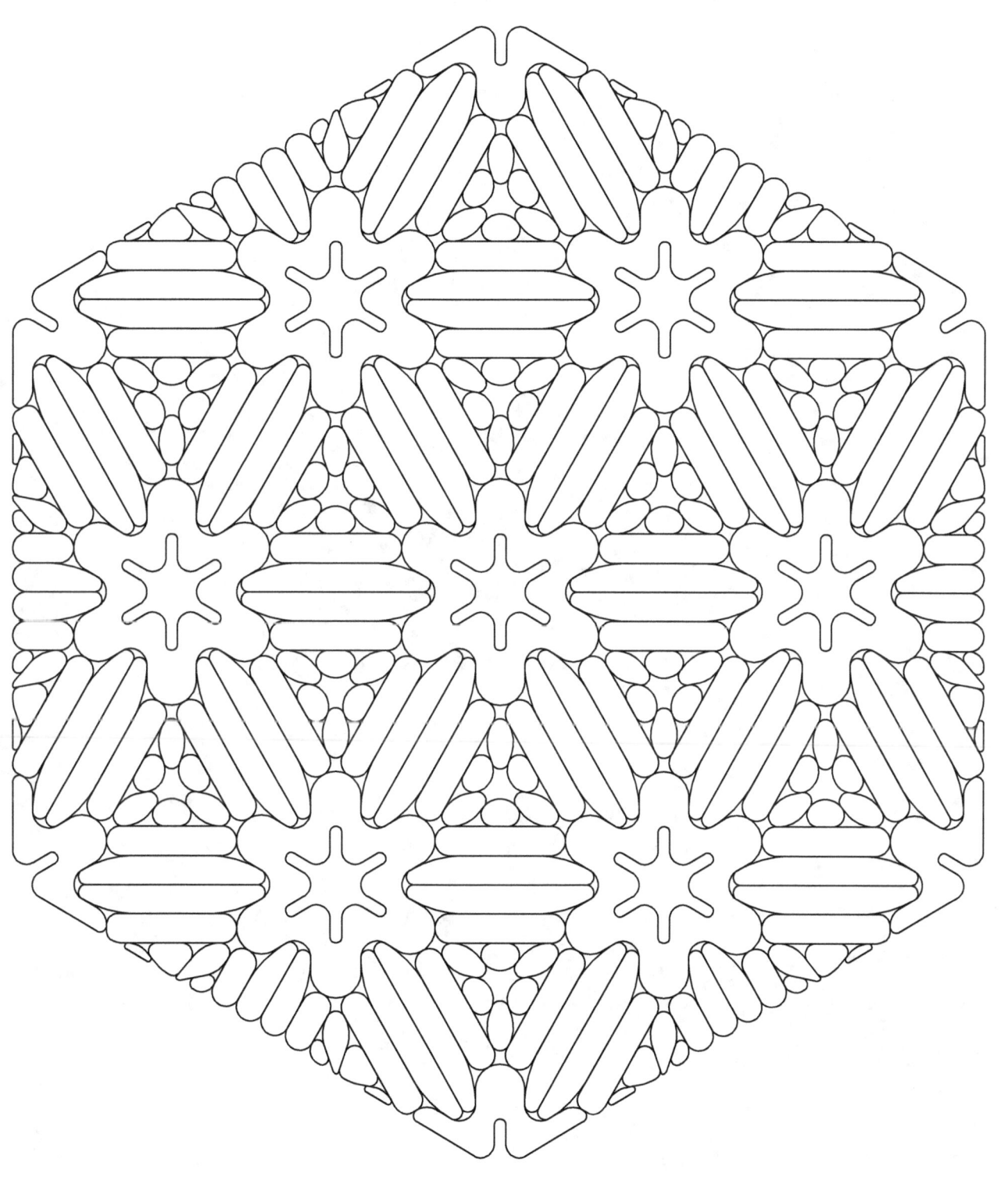

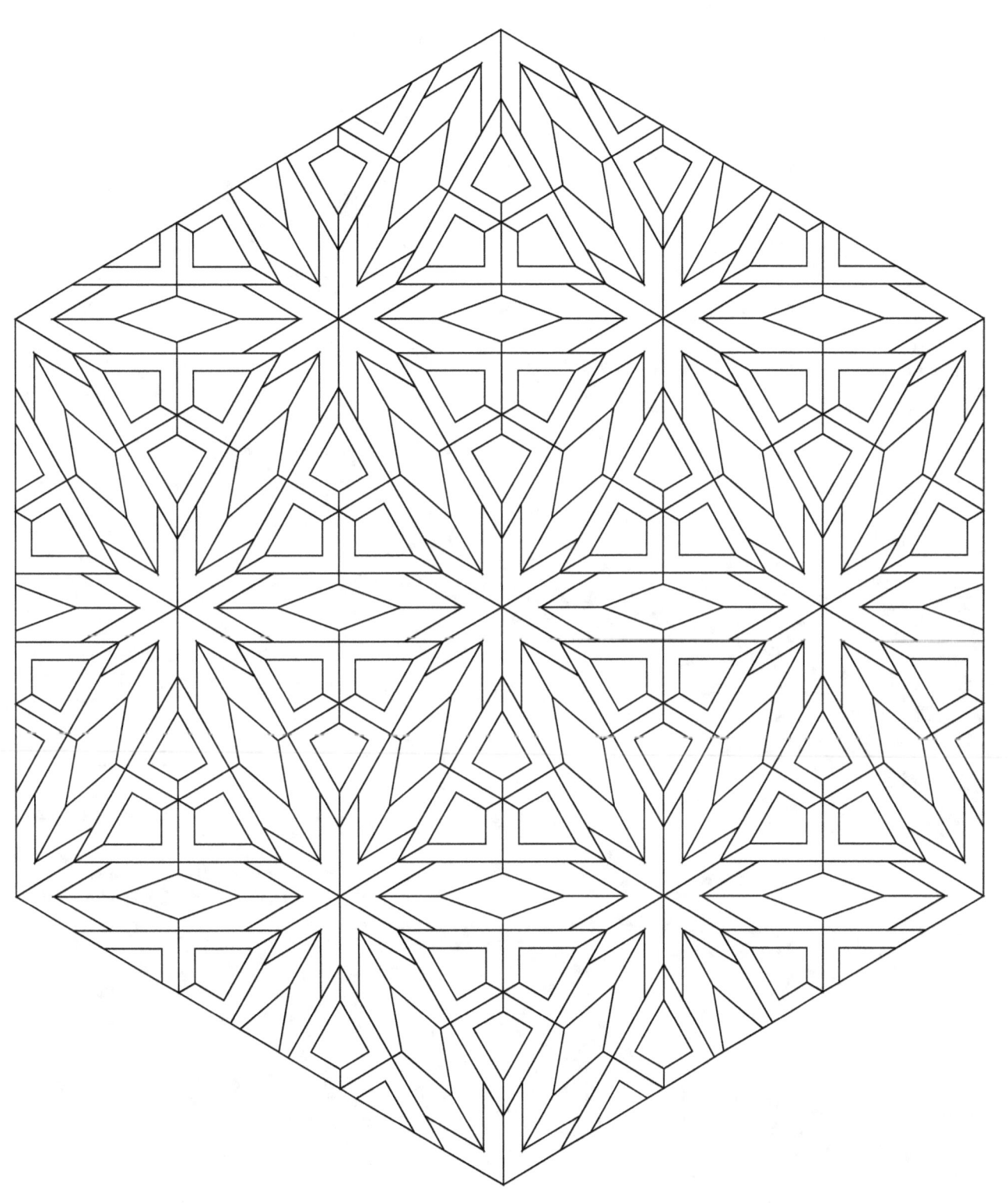

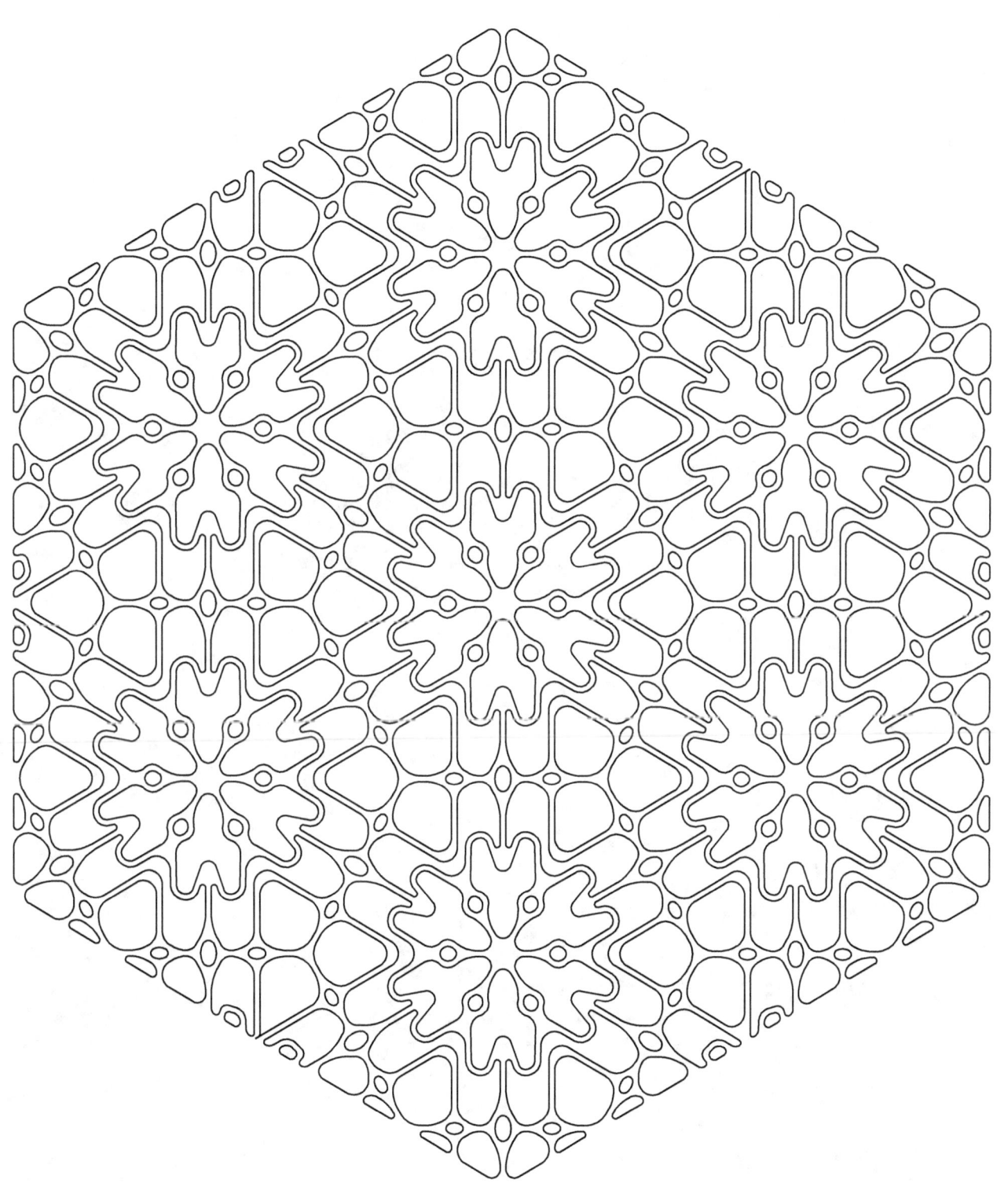

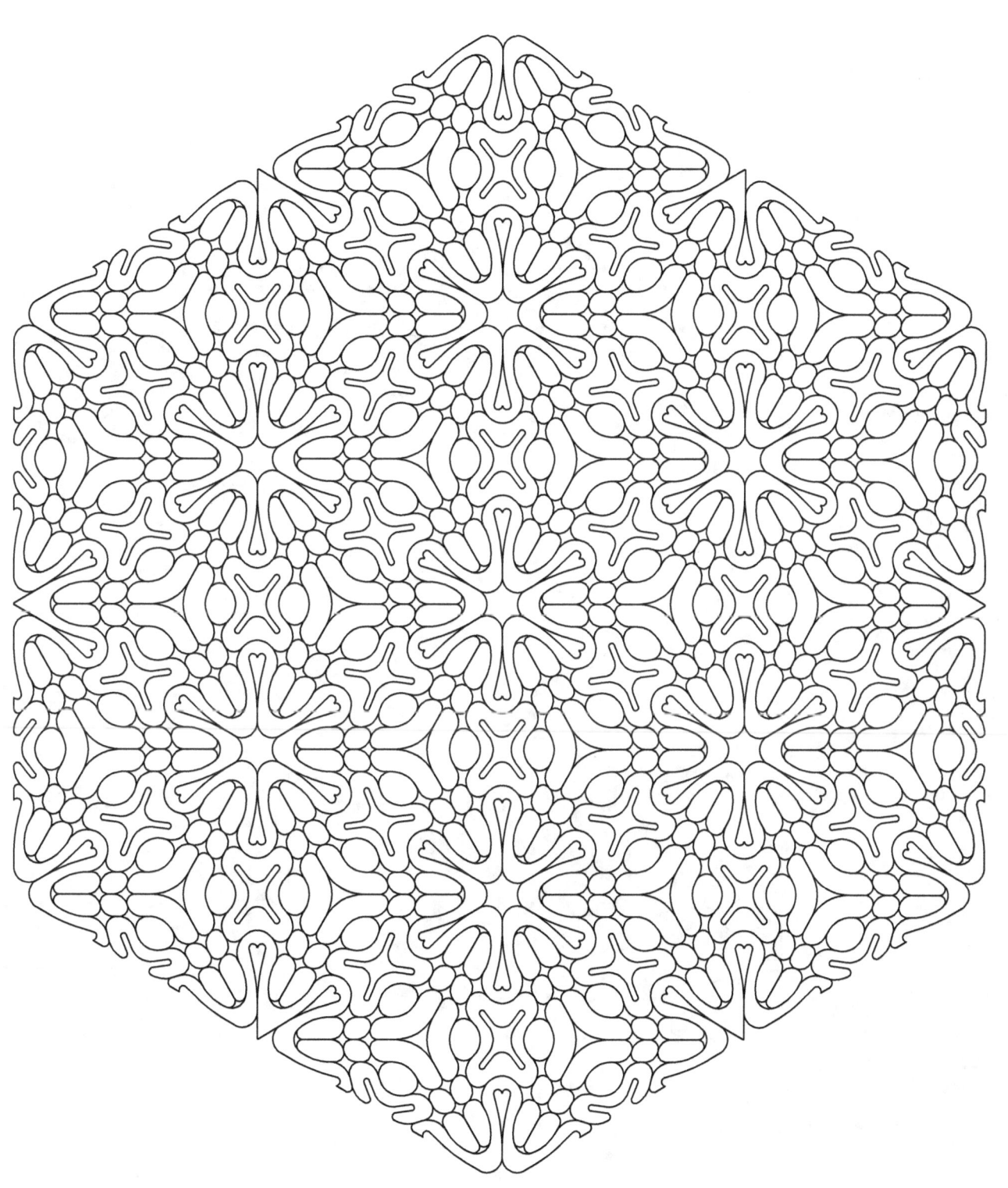

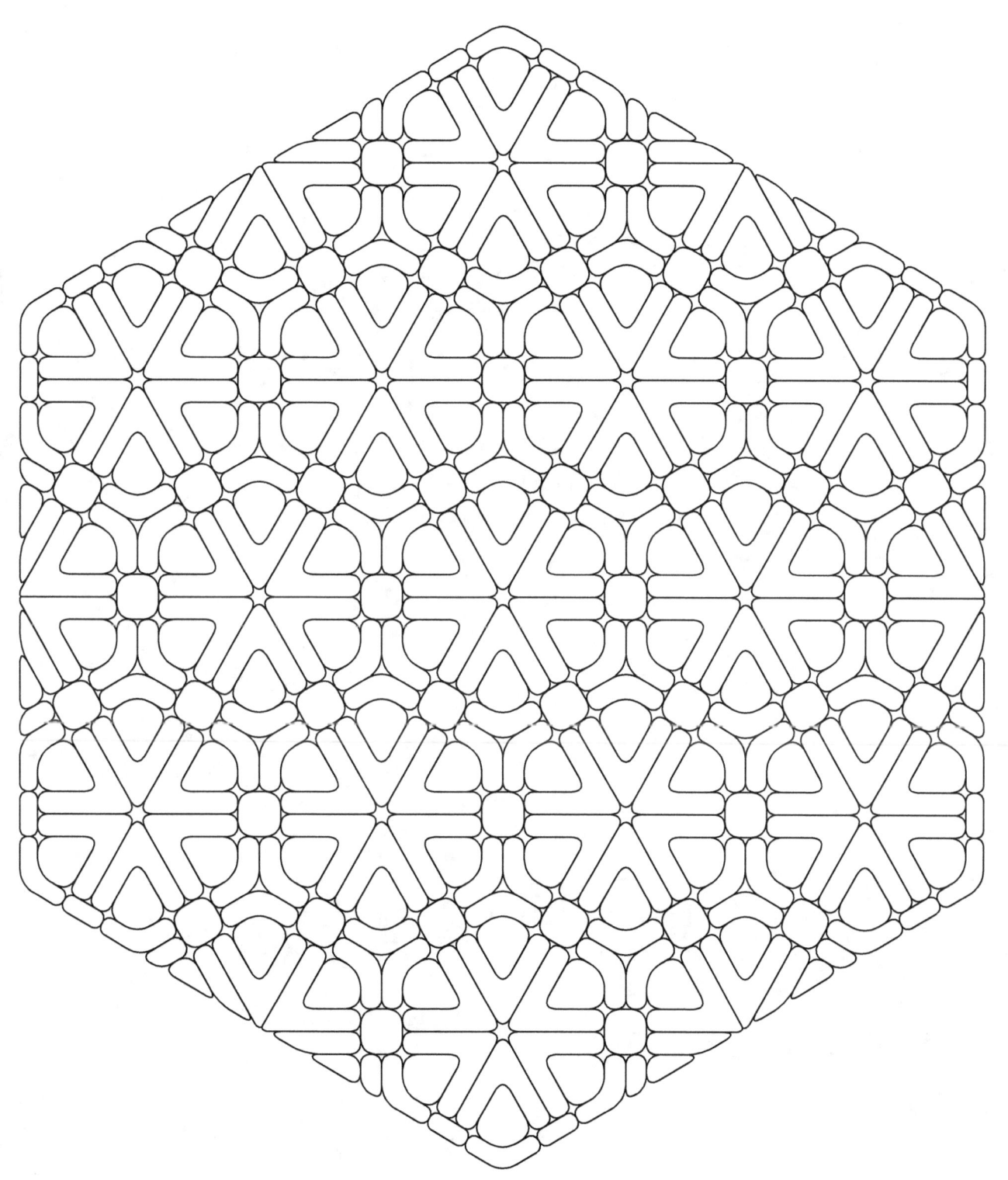

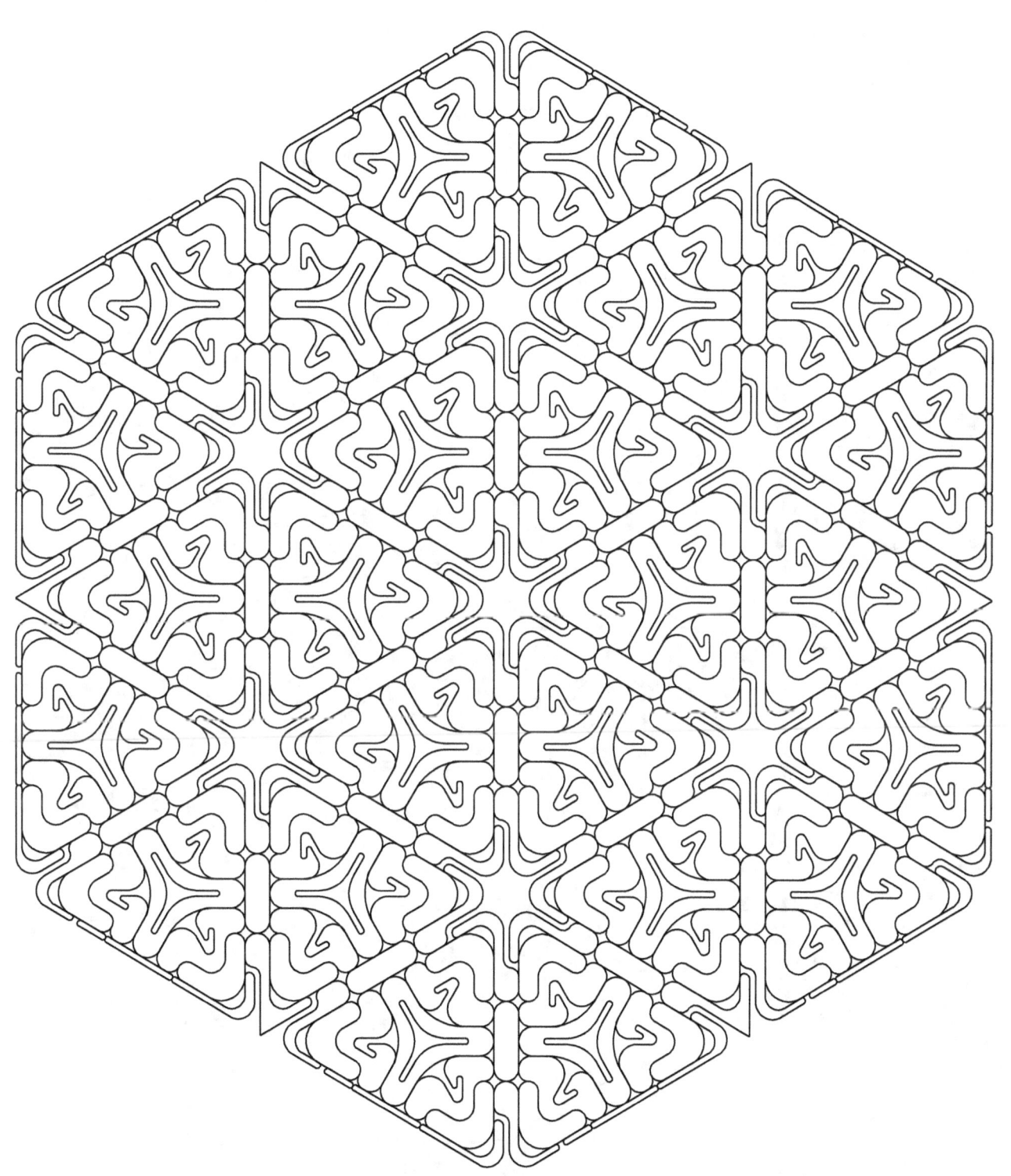

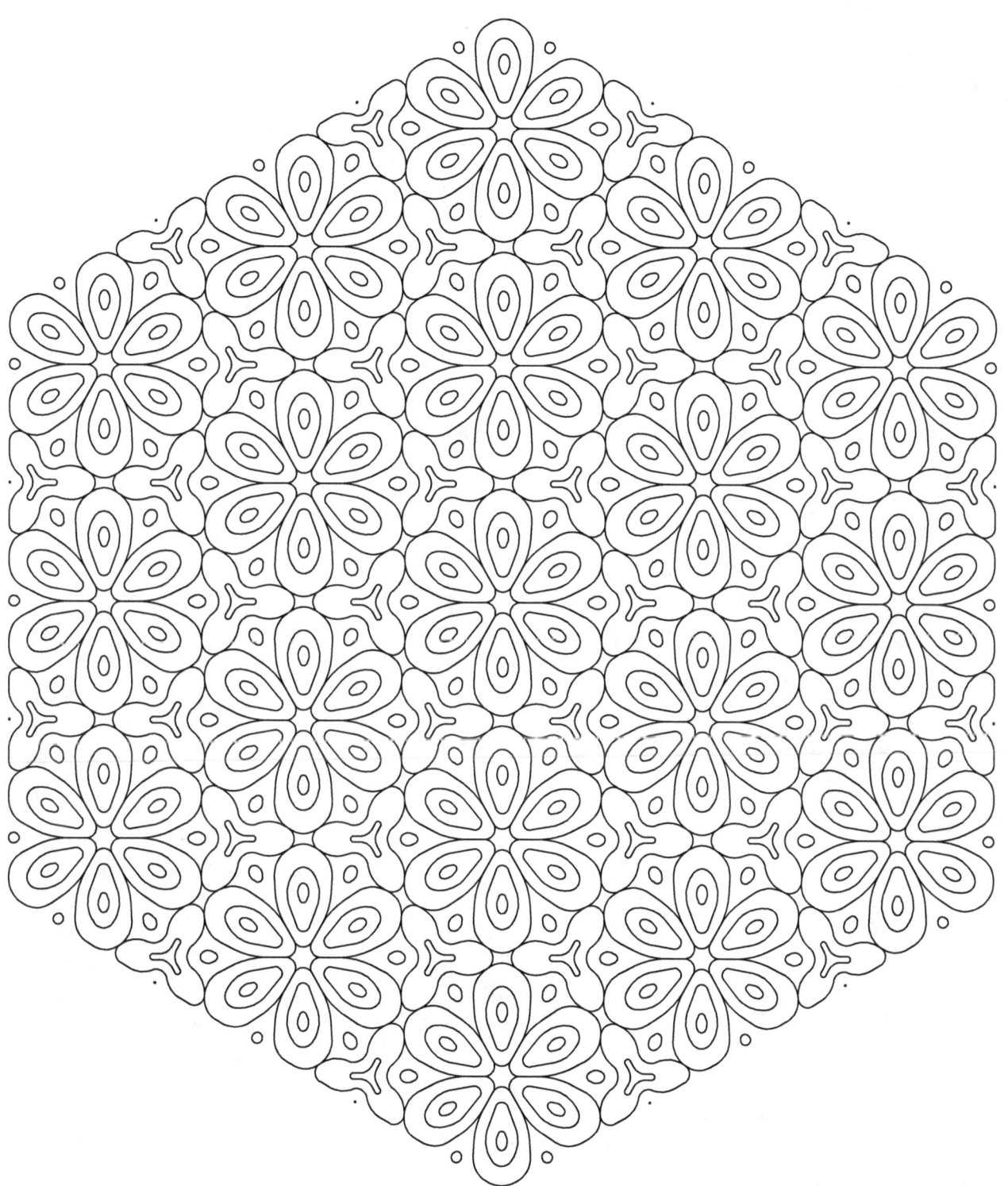

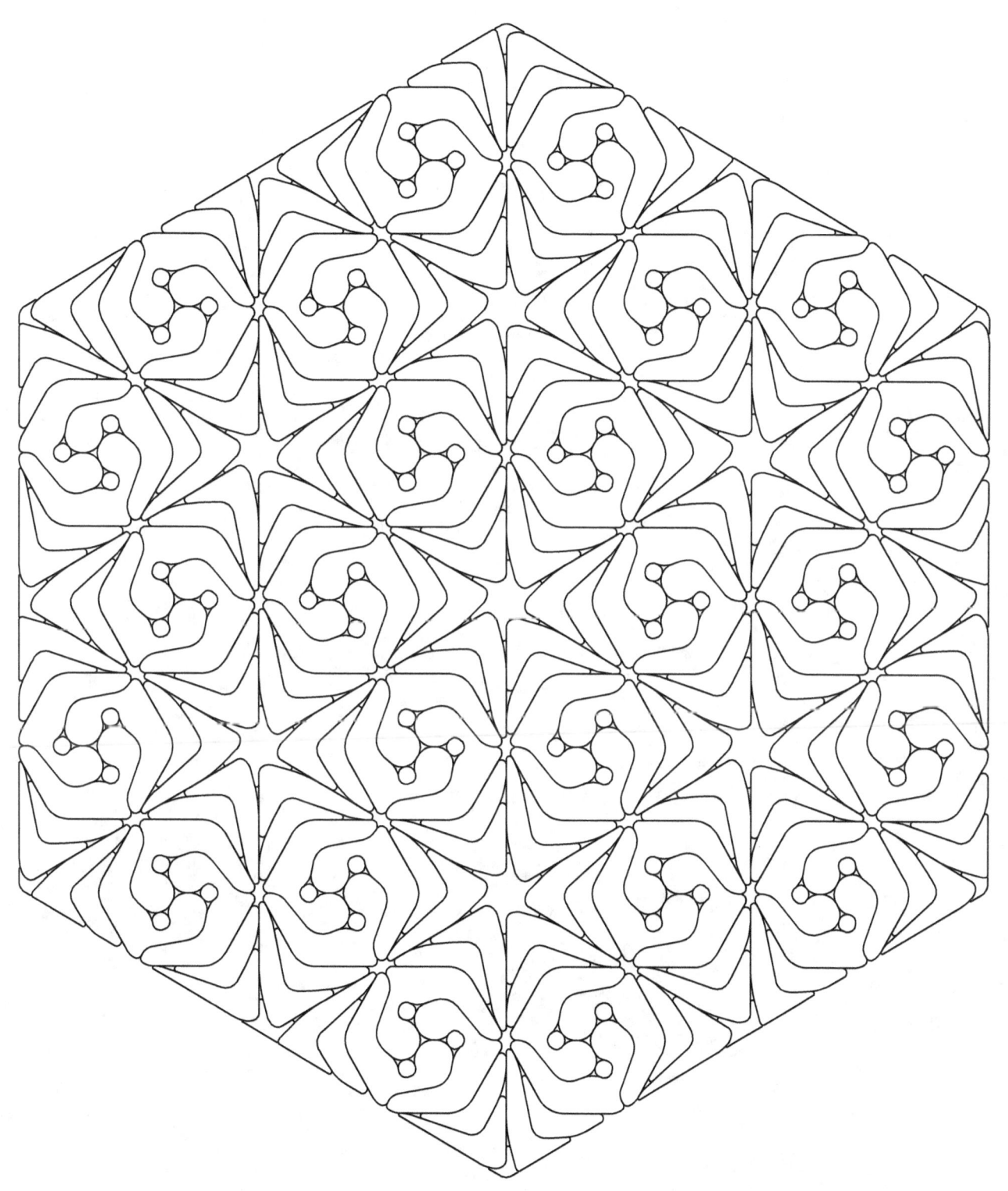

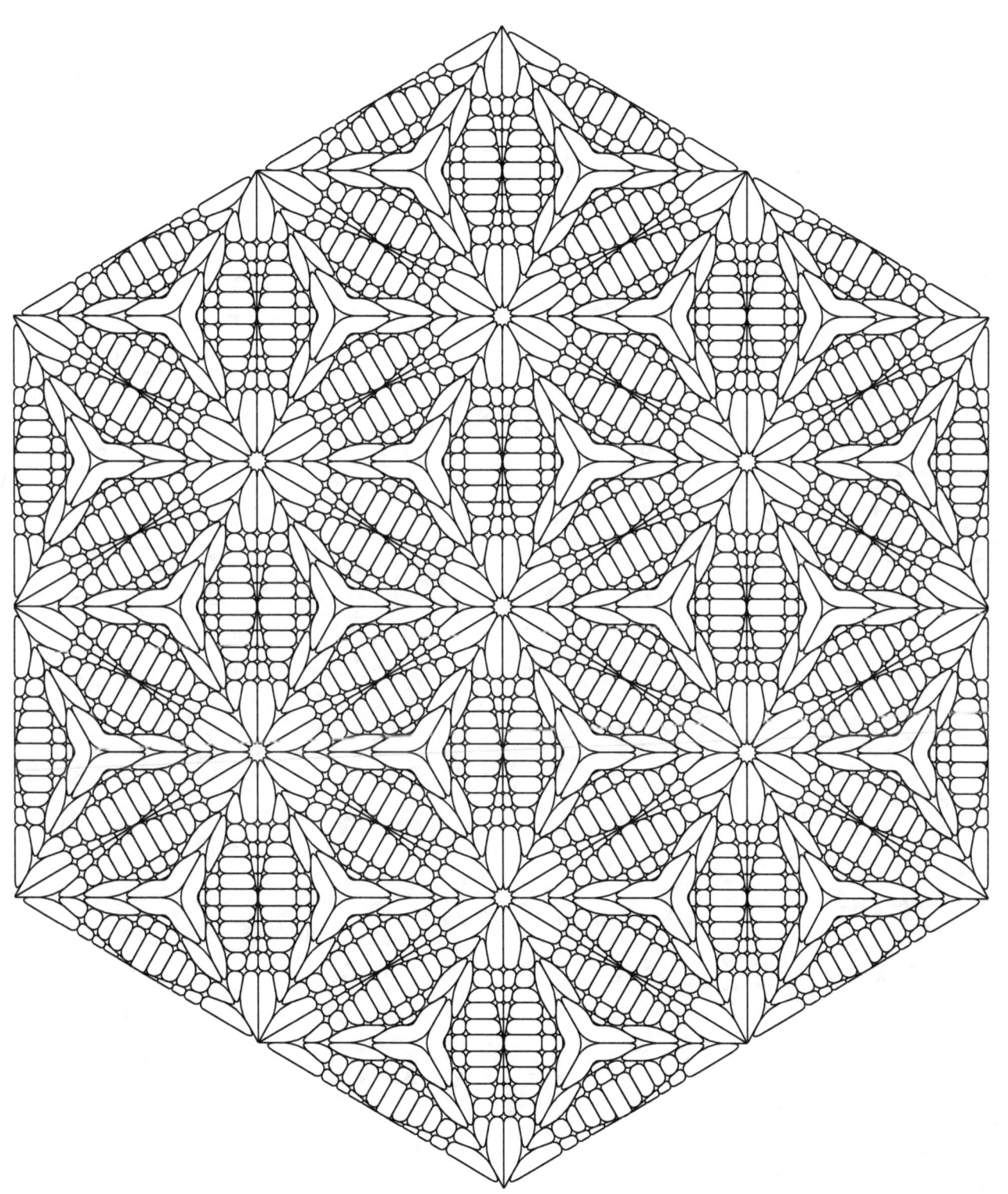

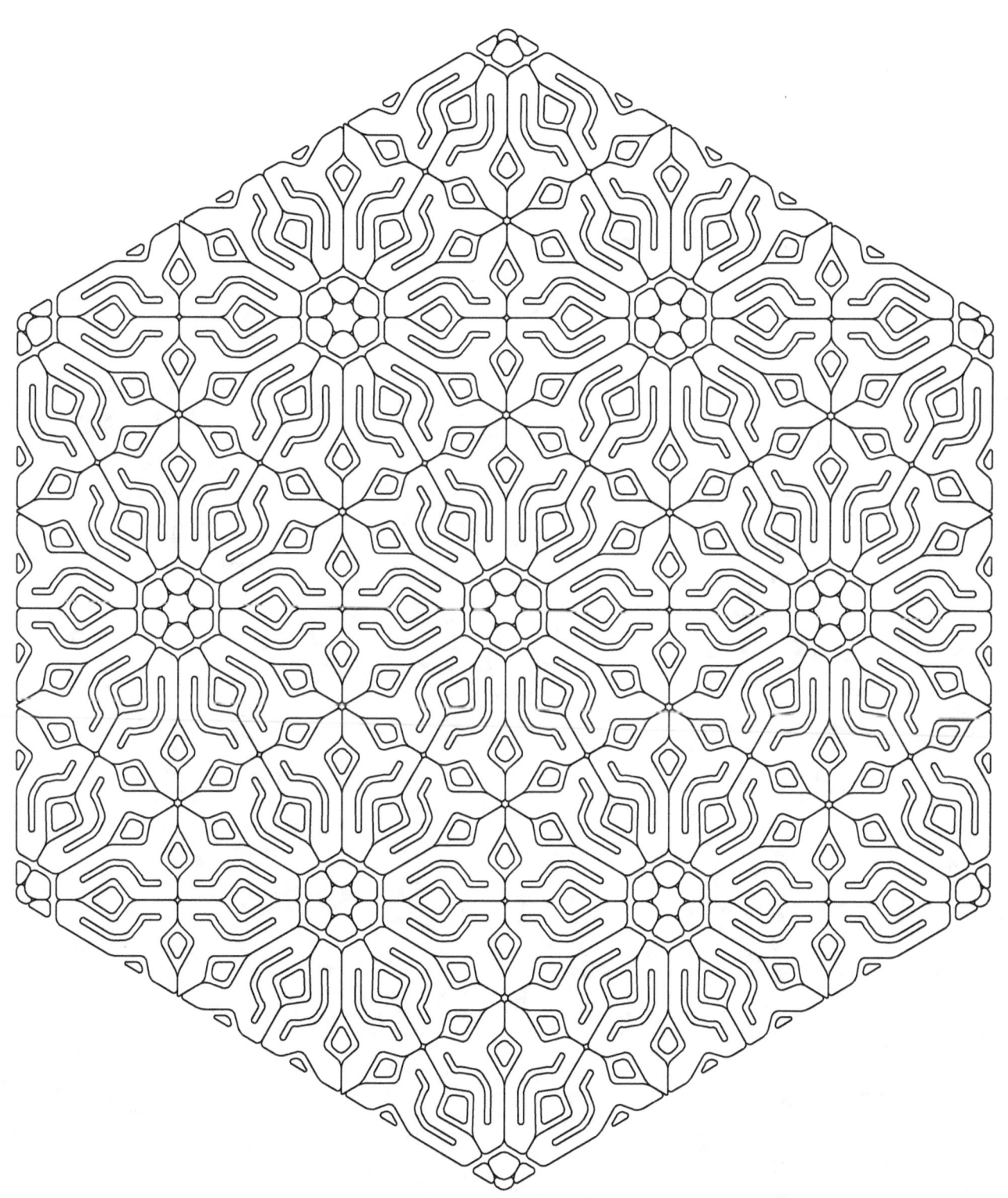

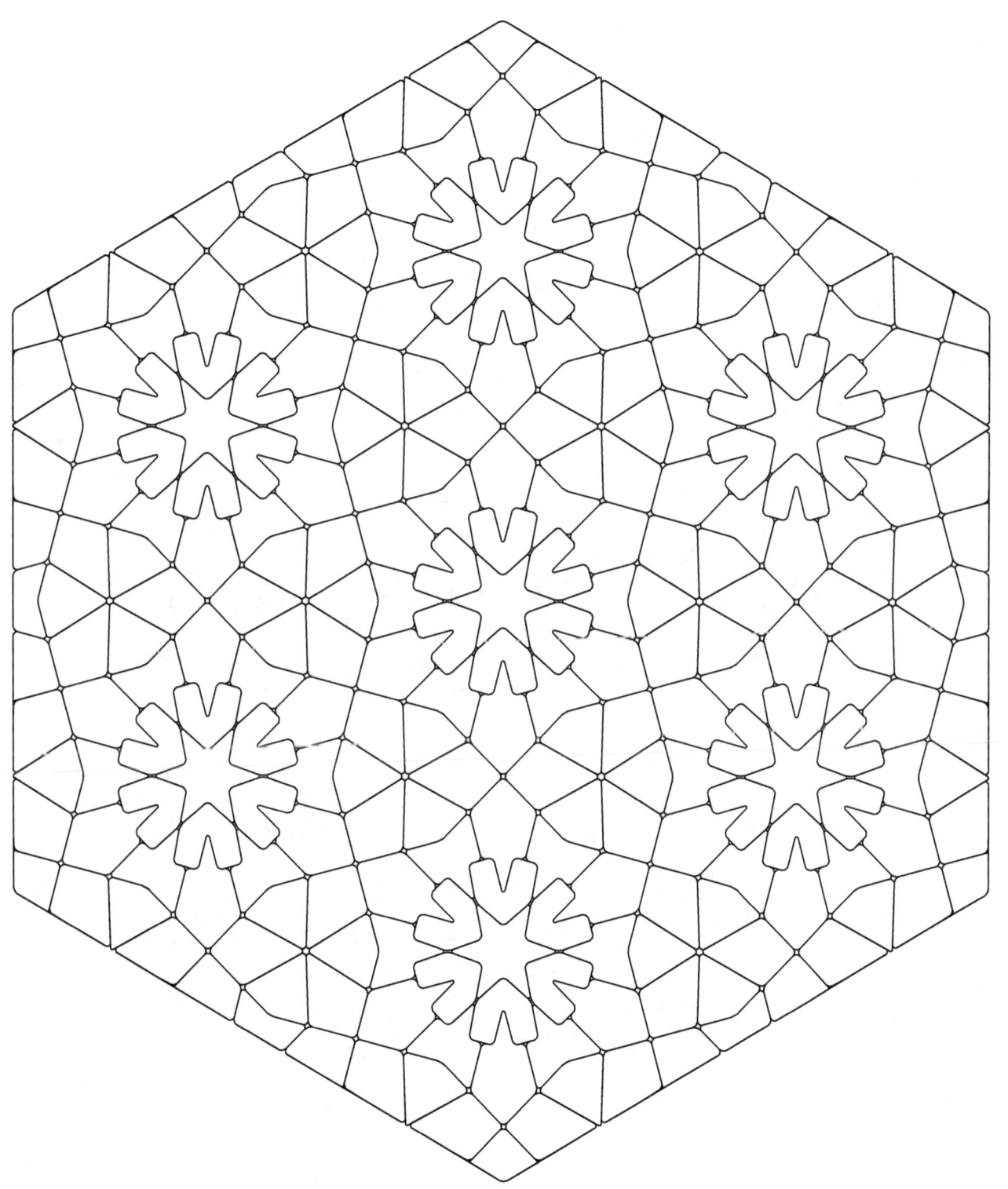

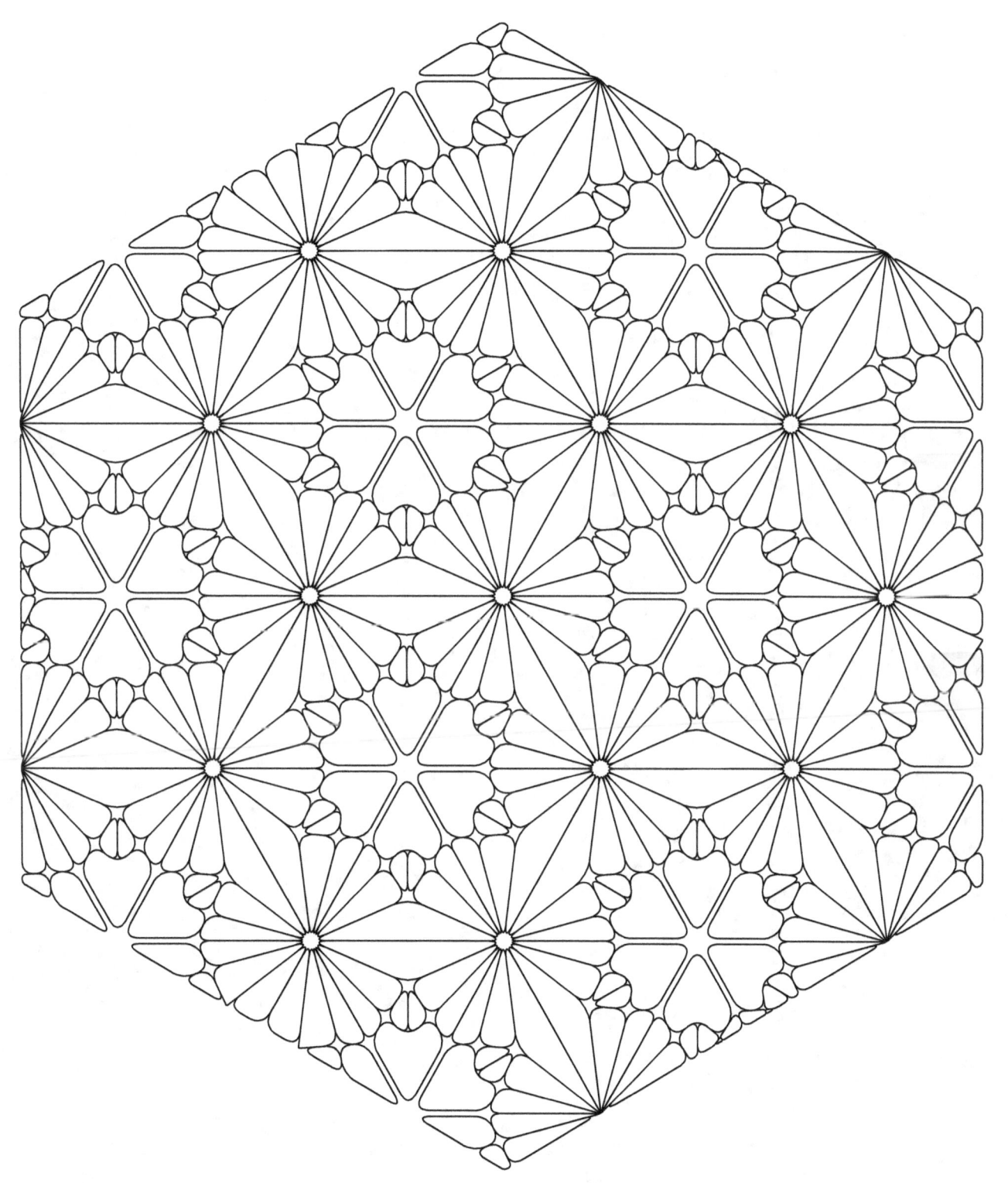

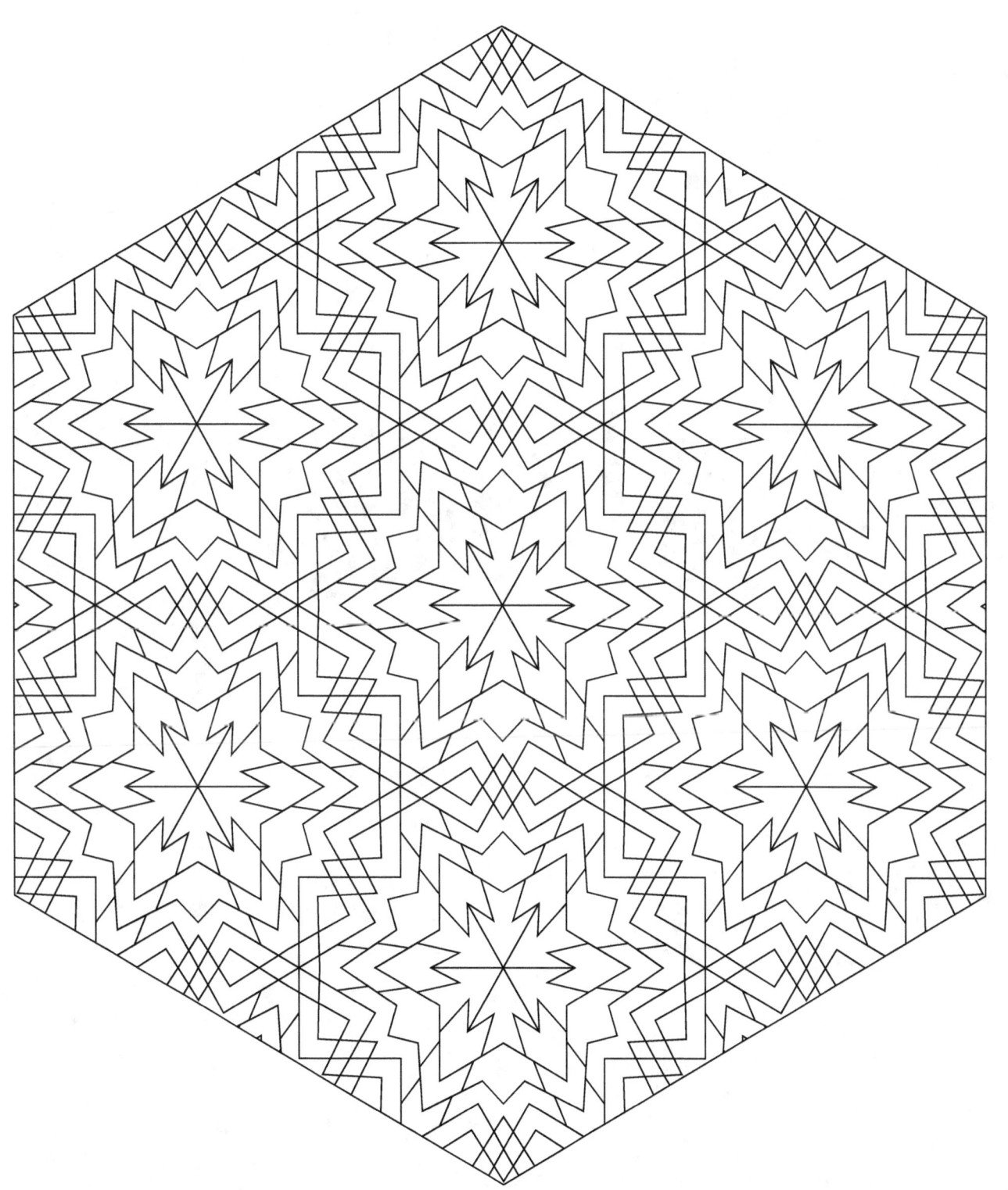

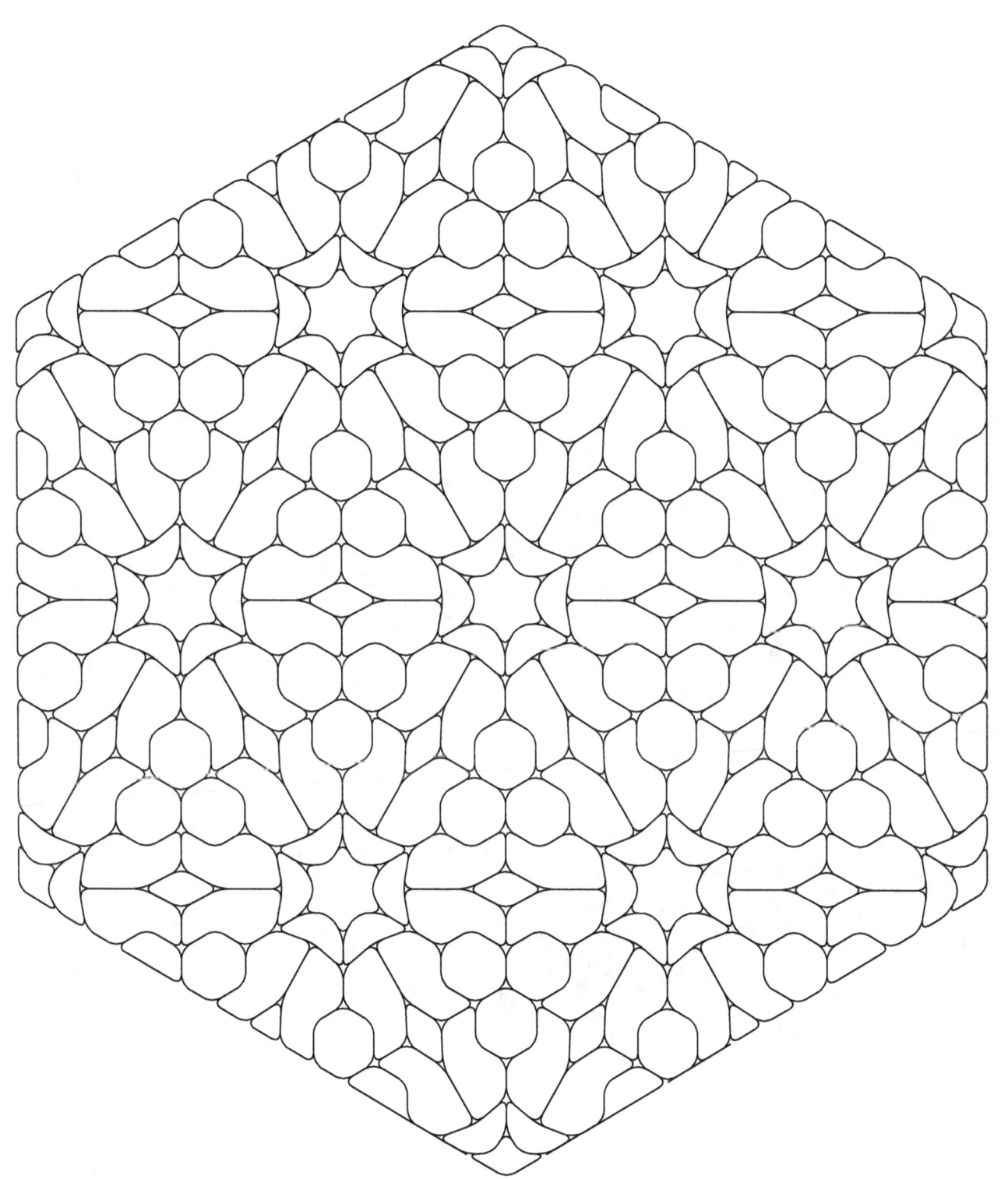

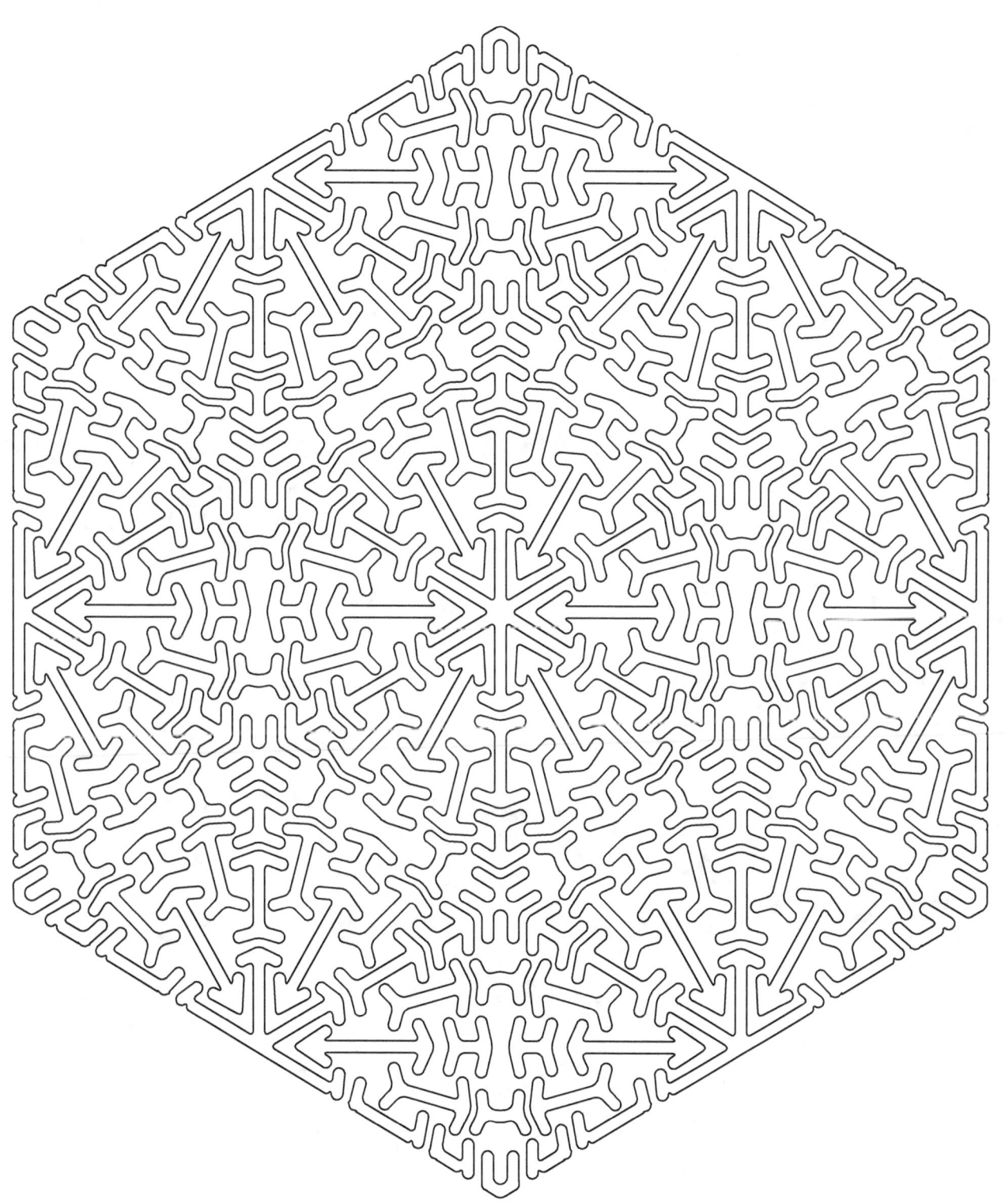

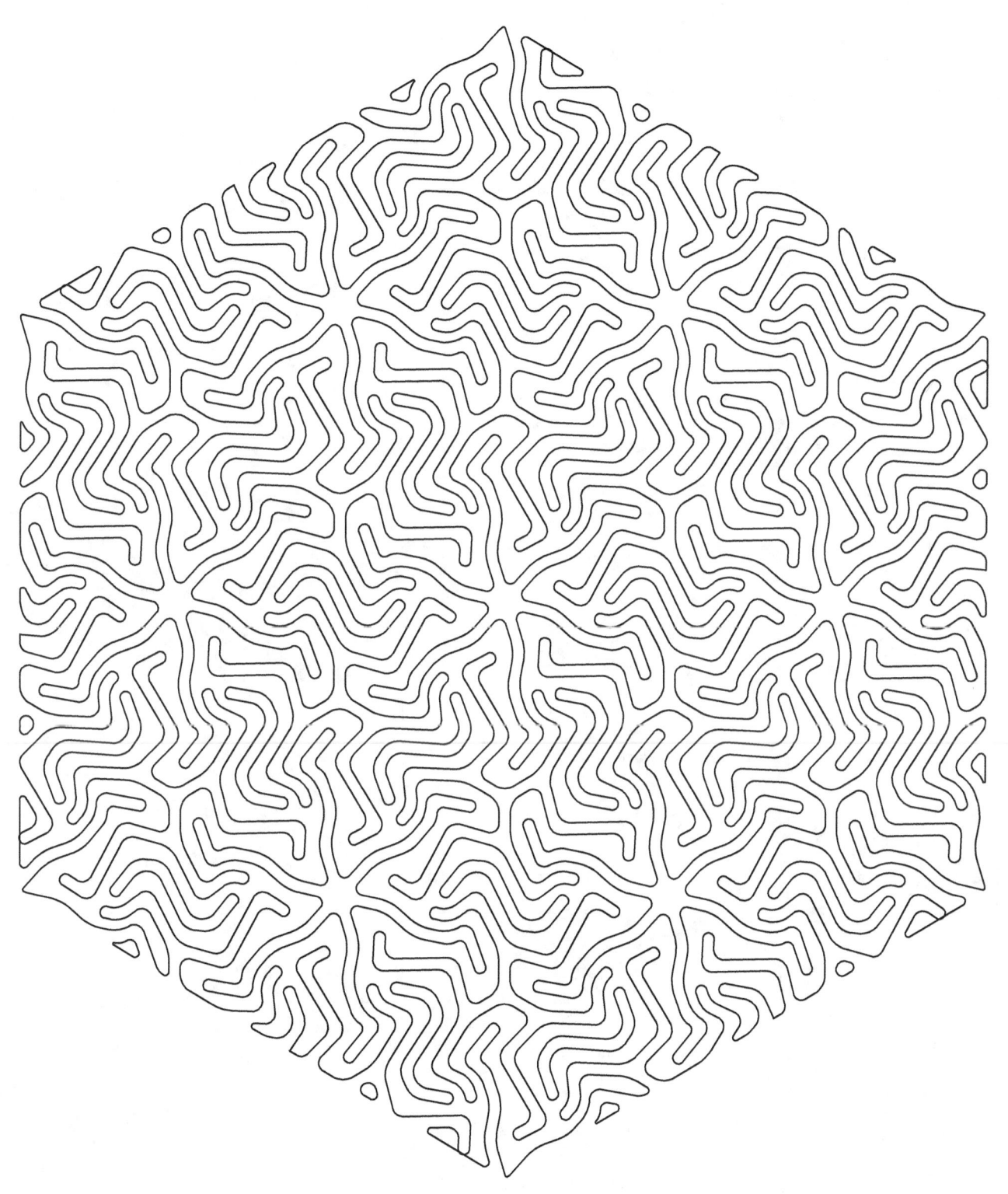

POLYGONIA DESIGNS

Hi! I hope you like the designs in this coloring book! I have had a lot of fun creating them. I have tried to include a variety, some simple, some more detailed, so you can find just the right one each time you want to sit and daydream.

You can find designs to download and other products to explore at

POLYGONIADESIGNS.COM

You can also sign up for a newsletter. And even learn how to make your own designs!

Designs by David Kaufman